Lisburn, Past and F

People, Places and Things

John Scott Hanna
Fredrick Gilbert Watson

W.J. BOYLE.
1885

If any there bee which are desirous to be strangers in their own soil and forrainers in their own citie, they may so continue, and therin flatter themselves. For such like I have not written these lines, nor taken these paines.

William Camden (1551–1623)

Published 2019 by Colourpoint Books
an imprint of Colourpoint Creative Ltd
Colourpoint House, Jubilee Business Park
21 Jubilee Road, Newtownards, BT23 4YH
Tel: 028 9182 6339
E-mail: sales@colourpoint.co.uk
Web: www.colourpoint.co.uk

First Edition
First Impression

A catalogue record for this book is available from the British Library.

Designed by April Sky Design, Newtownards
Tel: 028 9182 7195
Web: www.aprilsky.co.uk

Printed by W&G Baird Ltd, Antrim

ISBN 978 1 78073 261 9

Cover illustrations and frontispiece by Irish Linen Centre & Lisburn Museum
Front cover: Market Square, Lisburn. Steel engraving, circa 1865, drawn by J.H. Burgess – engraved by
Mould & Tod, Edinburgh, published by Marcus Ward, 6 Corn Market, Belfast.

Rear cover: Watercolour by David Gould (1871–1952) looking from the Market House towards Bow
Street, 1919. Gould, landscape painter from Scotland, came to Belfast in 1891 to learn damask
designing. He became an art teacher and taught for a time at Friends' School, Lisburn.

Frontispiece: Watercolour by W.J. Boyle, Market Square, Lisburn, dated 1885.

The support and co-operation of the Irish Linen Centre & Lisburn Museum
in the preparation of this book is gratefully acknowledged.

Contents

Foreword

IT IS PURE COINCIDENCE that Lisburn Museum should celebrate the fortieth anniversary of its foundation in the same year that *Lisburn, Past and Present – People, Places and Things*, a glimpse at local history, makes an appearance on the bookshelves. The Irish Linen Centre and Lisburn Museum intends to celebrate the occasion with an exhibition demonstrating its growth and development and our final selection of exhibits for that display will present a challenge similar to that faced by the authors in making their choice from a wide range of material.

In their case, John Hanna and Gilbert Watson solved the problem by including an interesting collection of men and women, who, having lived or passed through the wider Lisburn area, went on to make a major impact in their chosen field at home or abroad. As a museum professional I take pleasure in noting that in their selection our industrial linen heritage is still much to the fore in this the twenty-fifth anniversary of the formation of the Irish Linen Centre. This book refreshes our memory on local 'Places' that we perhaps take for granted and selects 'Things' acquired by the museum and places them in an historical context. With interesting subject matter and lots of illustrations *Lisburn, Past and Present – People, Places and Things* is a book to read and enjoy.

Paul Allison
Irish Linen Centre & Lisburn Museum

Introduction

W E INVITE YOU TO examine the imprint of history on the Lisburn area through a wide selection of people, places and things.

We start in the fresh air at the archaeological site at Duneight Motte and Bailey and the early settlement at Lissue Ringfort. The race meetings at the Maze next attract attention and we visit the Maze Racecourse where nobles of the land, church dignitaries and gentlemen jockeys were regular attenders. We hear of faction fights, robbery, personal attacks and even murder. At Kilwarlin, we meet with John Huss, the Protestant reformer, who preceded Martin Luther, and was burnt at the stake. His followers founded the 'Unitas Fratrum,' produced a hymn book in 1501 and the Kralitz Bible in 1579. Walk over the battlefield of the Battle of Thermopylae and encounter a Greek chieftain named Basil Patras Zula. Where? At Kilwarlin, outside Hillsborough. Back in Hillsborough village the Marquis of Downshire Memorial is a highly visible marker for a prominent landlord, who had the longest funeral procession in Ireland. Closer to the ground, a statue of the Fourth Marquis of Downshire, known as the 'Big Marquis,' was erected by his friends and family and stands in the centre of the village. In 1660, Charles II appointed Arthur Hill to be Hereditary Constable of Hillsborough Fort with twenty warders. Today the going rent for the Fort is one white rose payable to the Constable on his birthday! On a perimeter wall of the Fort, a stone plaque tells how the Irish Church Act deprived the Presbyterian Church of an endowment it had enjoyed for almost two centuries. The Regium Donum was granted by Charles II. King William III, he of 'glorious and immortal memory,' ordered a payment of £1,200. Queen Anne removed it before the close of her reign and George III was persuaded to reinstate it. Prime Minister Gladstone put an end to this Royal Bounty in 1869, but it still makes a contribution to today's salaries.

We leave Hillsborough, the birthplace of Sir Hamilton Harty, to the strains of one of his best-known songs, *My Lagan Love*. When the River Lagan was made navigable as far as Lisburn by building locks and straightening the course of the river, the *Lord Hertford* made the first voyage on the Lagan Navigation canal. An ambitious future scheme to see the Lagan Navigation reopened from Belfast Harbour to Lough Neagh will require exceptional funding. In the meantime, Navigation House at Sprucefield is being restored while the Union Locks erode and decay. Downstream at Lambeg, one of the impressive sights on the tow-path is Ballyskeagh High Bridge, arguably the most impressive canal bridge to survive in the Province. To the side of the bridge, before the invention of health and safety, a flight of steps led to The Lock-keeper's House. We visit Chrome Hill at the Wolfenden Bridge, to discover one of the few houses of character surviving in the Lisburn area. King William passed near here on his way to the Boyne in 1690 and John Wesley stopped there at a later date and left us the Wesley Tree.

We test your memory on the subject of Lisburn's industrial past. Do you remember Coulson's damask manufactory in Linenhall Street where the library now stands or the decaying shell of Hilden Mill where William Barbour & Sons started spinning flax in 1842. Is Stewart's Mill, which once employed 1,000 hands, a distant memory masked by Bow Street Mall? Can you remember the rambling brick structures of the Island Spinning Co. now replaced by a Civic Centre neatly dressed in Portland stone? Will you make the connection between Millbrook and Marks & Spencer in Donegall Place, Belfast? They link the firm of Richardson, Sons & Owden Ltd, a name synonymous with the linen industry in Ulster. All these manufacturers contributed to Lisburn's growth and prosperity as an Irish linen centre. From a range of linen industry experts we select Sir William McIlroy, a flax manager who spent his working life with William Barbour & Sons. He was a generous benefactor and a Papal Knight.

A colourful History in Stained Glass provides a look at local history as reflected in stained-glass windows in local churches. Lambeg graveyard is the resting place of the Rev. Saumarez Dubourdieu, a gentleman forced into exile by religious persecution, who earned for himself on merit, a name, a habitation and a new country among strangers. An interesting story of Huguenot endeavour.

We trace the history of the game of golf in Lisburn from 1890, on the first tee at Manor House Golf Club, to the move to Blaris and the establishment of Lisburn Golf Club. Step out into the historic green space that is Wallace Park, the gift of Sir Richard Wallace in 1885, for the enjoyment of the good citizens of the town – 'The People's Park'. From Glenavy we follow Miss Laura Bell on her path to glory from prostitution in Belfast, her brief encounters with Sir William Wilde in Dublin, a Nepalese prince in London and her friendship with Prime Minister Gladstone. Her marriage to Captain Thistlethwayte, her conversion and popular evangelical tea parties in Grosvenor Square are in sharp contrast.

Travel on the section of railway line from Belfast to Lisburn, which was officially opened by the Ulster Railway Company in 1839, when over 3,000 people made the journey. Rebuilt in 1878, for the Great Northern Railway Co., Lisburn Station deserves a second look.

When it opened in 1890, the Lisburn Temperance Institute was, in effect, a Victorian community centre, providing a meeting place for townspeople and visitors. The building serves the same purpose today as the Bridge Community Centre. We examine the provision of medical care in the days before the much-maligned National Health Service and provide a glimpse of the service offered by the County Antrim Infirmary and an 'interesting if lurid account' of conditions in the 1800s. We find what conditions were like for the inmates of Lisburn Workhouse from its opening in 1841, with 250 paupers, until it closed its doors in 1922. We view history in a few 'Things'. History notices a local connection with the Belfast Harp Society, and a generous donation to the Lisburn Museum of the Egan Harp in 2002, enriched that heritage. The purchase of Captain Nickerson's Watch focused attention on the plight of the cotton weavers from the Maze, Broomhedge and Lisburn areas in 1863–64 and the efforts made to relieve their sufferings.

Famous people with Lisburn roots or connections attract our attention. From his home at Ravarnette, we follow Robert Hart on a career path that led to his appointment as Inspector-General of the Chinese Imperial Maritime Customs. A workaholic, this became his life work. Famed in China, but largely forgotten at home, a memorial to Sir Robert Hart stands in Blaris Old Cemetery. Originally from Lissue, Alexander Turney Stewart left behind modestly comfortable beginnings to establish in New York the largest retail store in the world. He gave largely to charity and also remembered the needs at home. John Ballance from Glenavy was acknowledged to be a man of great honesty and integrity, who served as Prime Minister of New Zealand and earned lasting respect as a reforming, enlightening and accomplished politician. Samuel McCloy from Bridge Street, the talented subject and landscape painter, was Master of the Waterford School of Art and exhibited his work in Dublin and London. His work is much sought after. Brigadier-General John Nicholson, soldier, statesman and hero, who fell mortally wounded at the siege and storming of Delhi, was worshiped by fakirs as the great god Nikalsain. On plaques mounted on the base of Nicholson's statue we learn of the deeds of valour of Corporal William James Lendrim VC and Sergeant Samuel Hill VC. In 1903, Field-Marshal Lord Roberts fulfilled a personal wish to visit Lisburn, believing it to be the birth place of General Nicholson, on whose staff he once served. To commemorate the visit, he planted Lord Roberts' Oak in Castle Gardens and confused the press corps.

Lieutenant William Dobbs, son of the Rector of Lisburn Cathedral and a married man of three days standing, was mortally wounded while taking part in a naval battle against the celebrated pirate Paul Jones in Carrickfergus Bay in 1778. His memory is cut in marble in the Cathedral and a ballad describes the sea battle. Brigadier John Alexander Sinton VC has the unique distinction of being the only holder of the Victoria Cross who was also a Fellow of the Royal Society. The 1908 wedding album of the year belonging to Thomas Andrews and Helen Reilly Barbour provides Lambeg's link to Thomas Andrews, Harland & Wolff and the ill-fated Titanic. Miss Barbour is ably supported by bridesmaids in Bo-Peep costumes.

The annals of history are marked with battles, as is the Lisburn War Memorial. One hundred years ago the armistice on the Western Front came into force on 11 November 1918 but The Treaty of Versailles was not signed until June 1919. In Lisburn, on Peace Day, 16 August 1919, a wooden cenotaph was erected in Market Square and we learn how near we were to losing the war. During World War II the Long Kesh Airfield and the other Lisburn airfields were designed to be able to respond to a possible German invasion of the United Kingdom through the 'back door.' The airfield hangars survive as a museum. We are grateful for another survivor, Professor Frank Pantridge, who served with the Royal Army Medical Corps during the fall of Singapore, and survived the horrors of captivity in a Japanese labour camp. He went on, in an outstanding medical career, to transform emergency medicine with the invention and development of the portable defibrillator.

This is all part of the rich tapestry of Lisburn's history, which is on view as you turn the pages of this book. This travelogue through local history is designed to hold your interest and intended as a good read.

Duneight Motte and Bailey

The bailey, the Ravarnet River forming the southern boundary.

DUNEIGHT MOTTE AND BAILEY is located in north-west Co. Down, between the Ravarnet river and the road leading from Ravarnet village to Legacurry Presbyterian Church. This site, which is in State Care, has been used and remodelled on several occasions, extending from the Bronze Age to the Norman conquest of Ulster. Its shape is that of a triangular motte, with a bailey on the east, surrounded by a continuous ditch except to the south, where there is a steep slope down to the river. The ridge on which the bailey stands was first used by Bronze Age people as a grave site for the cremated remains of a human adult, contained in a collared urn, accompanied by two flint tools.

The site was first occupied permanently by the native Irish at some period from possibly the tenth to the early twelfth century. Within the fortified enclosure, evidence of at least three wooden or stone buildings has been discovered. It is probable that this settlement may be the Dun-Echdach mentioned in the *Annals of Ulster*. In 1003, at the battle of Craebh-telcha, between the Oulipians and Cinel-Eoghain, the Elidia's were defeated. The fighting is said to have 'extended to Dun Echdach, and to Druim Bó' (the Ridge of the Cow) – the present Drumbo, with the remains of its round tower, lies four miles north-east of the present townland of Duneight. Seven years later, in 1010, the *Annals* record a hosting by Flaithbertach Ua Neill to Dun-Echdach, when he burned down the dun (or fort), and broke down the town (baile), and brought pledges from Niall, son of Dubhtuinne.

The site was converted for use as a motte and bailey castle in the late twelfth – early thirteenth century by the Anglo-Normans. In addition to the construction of the motte in the eastern section of the bailey, the latter's bank was also enlarged at this time, and the approach to the fort was altered to allow entry through a gate adjacent to the motte. There are no documentary references to Duneight in Norman times. The castle would have served as the northern link of a chain of motte and bailey fortresses – Sheeptown, Ballyroney, Dromore, spread out through west Down on the flank of the English holding in south-east Ulster. Records of Royal expenditure 1211–12 at Ballyroney and Dromore emphasise the importance attached to these castles, all of which probably date from the early years of the English settlement.

Duneight Motte and Bailey.
(JSH)

Lissue Ringfort

THIS ARCHAEOLOGICAL SITE IS situated three miles from Lisburn at Cross Lane just off the Moira Road. It lies in the townland of Lissue. In place-names, two words commonly refer to ringforts. The first is Rath, the anglicised form of the Irish ráith, meaning an 'earthen bank' and the other is Lis, Irish lios, meaning a 'courtyard' or 'enclosure'. This is the first part of the townland name Lissue, Irish 'Lios-Áedha', 'the fort of (a person called) Aed.'

As Richard Warner explains, from the archaeological excavations undertaken by Dr Gerhard Bersu, it seems that there was a small ringfort on this site before the construction of the one which is now visible. This second much larger ringfort was completely filled by a single huge building, some 130 feet in diameter. Artefacts found at this site produced a large amount of the 'souterrain' pottery, a bronze pin, some iron objects, two glass beads and a fragment of a bronze ladle. The most spectacular find was a slab of slate covered with carefully drawn incised sketches: an animal, bits of interlaced, geometric patterns. Other findings indicate that the total structure was eventually destroyed by fire. Usefully it can be approximately dated to about A.D. 1000 by the ornaments carved on it.

This ringfort was much larger than most of the others and people expected to have a house of this size were a king and a hosteller. There is some evidence to support each of these possibilities. A hosteller was a wealthy member of society whose function was to provide accommodation for travellers. The hostel building would have been substantial and would probably have been a separate establishment from the hosteller's farm. It was usually close to roads or a river crossing. There was probably a crossing of the river Lagan near here. The ring-fort is on the opposite side of the river from the early Christian monastery at Blaris.

On the other hand, there could be a royal explanation. By the 9th century one dynastic line had its capital at Dun Echdach, Duneight in Co. Down. In A.D. 882 Ainbíth, a powerful king of the Ulaid, and a member of the Dun Echdach dynasty died. He is credited in an early genealogical tract with having founded the 'family of Lisaeda', that is the 'family of the fort of Aed', Aed being his father. We cannot be certain that the Lios Áedha in which this family lived was this Lissue, but it seems probable. Seemingly unnoticed and surrounded by commercial and manufacturing premises, archaeological excavations have shown that Lissue ringfort is a remarkable site with an unusual history and possible royal status, a site well worth preserving and worth a visit.

A typical ringfort

The Maze Racecourse

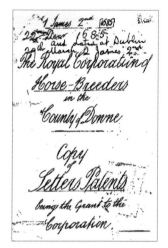

Copy of Letters Patent.
(Down Royal)

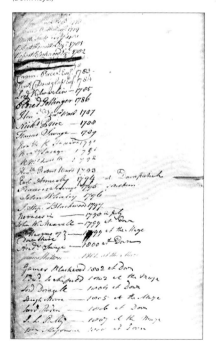

Down Royal members dating from 1782.
(Down Royal)

DOWN ROYAL, THE RACECOURSE at the Maze, just outside Lisburn, is the location for the premier horse racing events in Ulster. Since the eighteenth century the Sport of Kings has thrilled generations of visitors to this rural townland. The peace and tranquillity normally associated with the quiet fields that stretch along the river Lagan would regularly be disturbed by the bustle and throng of people attending the race-meetings. The tenant farmers on the Cockhill Road and Dunnygarton Lane would have been subjected to the influx of visitors and travellers from all over Ireland converging on the racecourse. On main roads and by-roads, they came on horse and on foot and in all types of transport from splendid coaches, gigs and traps to the tradesman's cart specially fitted up for the occasion. Dunnygarton Lane meandered through the course itself and it is easy to imagine the carnival atmosphere that would prevail on the occasion of a holiday in the general area with excitement for rich and poor alike. Farmer, weaver, artisan and labourer would mingle with the gentry on these great occasions as they headed for the colourful flag bedecked tents of the stewards, saddlers, fortune tellers, gambling side shows and taverns.

The origins of the course are much older, as a patent to establish a Corporation of Horse-breeders for Down had been granted by James II in 1685, the objective being the encouragement of horse breeding in the County of Down, and a racecourse at Downpatrick had been formed in 1685. Under the Royal Charter the Corporation had a number of duties including the annual running of a six-day horse fair preceding the running of their Annual Plate. The Corporation also had the power to hold a Court of Py Pounder during the fairs and all subsequent race meetings. When William III visited Hillsborough Castle as the guest of William Hill he issued a letter to Christopher Carleton, the Collector of Customs at Belfast, granting £100 to be known as the King's Plate, to be competed for at Hillsborough. William Hill established the course at the Maze and his heir, the Right Honourable Michael Hill, implemented improvements and took a keen interest in racing blood stock.

Racing commenced at the Maze site in the early 1700s with the Governor and the Freemen resolving that a plate for five-year-olds be run every third Thursday in June. The horses had to be trained in County Down or by a member of the Corporation. They were to carry 10 stone 1 pound with a prize fund of £70. There followed a number of races which reflected the rivalry between Lord Antrim, Lord Rawdon and Lord Massereene. In 1750, King George II donated £100 to run the King's Plate and to the present day a race named Her Majesty's Plate is run in July over 1 mile 5 furlongs, with the prize money contributed to by the Privy

Purse. Walter Harris, writing in 1744, gives us a brief description of the course:

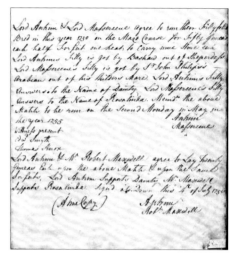

Down Royal Match Book listing races which took place in 1750 and 1755.
(Down Royal)

> The Maze-Course, a place set apart for the publick diversions of horse racing, is upwards of a mile north of the town, near the banks of the River Lagan. A rising hill in the middle of the course, about two miles in circumference, gives the spectators a full view of the whole field, and on the top of the hill a wooden tower is erected, open on all sides, for spectators to sit and view the course.

This original tower or stand referred to by Harris was a wooden structure, but it was replaced by a round white-washed stone tower on Tower Hill. The hill formed a natural vantage point for the spectators and in earlier times it was not unusual for them to cut a flat hearth into the slope and cook over a lighted fire while they viewed the races. The slope of the ground was the cause of many a fall as the crowd surged forward with excitement to see the closing stages of a race. Just before the races in July 1775, Mr. Perfect, an itinerant Methodist minister preached at nearby Halftown and during the sermon warned his congregation not to attend the racecourse, which was the scene of so many crimes and numerous calamities. The following eye-witness account is provided by local man Patrick Cunningham, who ignored the warning (horse racing being his favourite sport) but refrained from attending the Sunday races. He records:

> The first day of the races presented a most shocking scene perhaps not less than one hundred thousand people all confusion and uproar. This was occasioned by a quarrel between the men of Broomhedge and those of Hillsborough. They armed themselves with whatever weapons they could get, and rushed upon each other with the ferocity of wild beasts, and fought with the greatest desperation. Such rage and clamour I never witnessed before. In a little time many of them were weltered in their own blood. I remember one only killed on the spot, but several died afterwards of their wounds.

Faction fights were not new to the area. The men of Broomhedge and Maze were known to fight over the right to cut turf in Donnygarton bog. Patrick Cunningham's assessment of the crowd is questionable, but the racecourse was at its peak in attendance terms between 1811 and 1825. The course was at times graced by men of prominence and distinction. Lord Castlereagh, with his retinue and friends, paid it occasional visits. The Marquis of Downshire, Marquis of Donegall, Lords Portarlington and O'Neill, and many such noblemen; Colonel Sparrow of Tandragee Castle; Colonel Cope of Loughgall, J.W. Maxwell, Nicholas Price, Colonel Forde, Sir S. May, Sir Robert Bateson, the Messrs Whaley, McCance, Savage, Batt, Verner, Greg, Martin, Fivey, Moore, Nugent, Hall and Shaw; indeed, nearly every man of note in the province thronged the scene with a splendid array of carriages.

Maze racecourse,
3 August 1852.
(Watercolour by James Moore,
1819–1883)

James Watson on his
favourite horse 'Johnny'.
(FGW)

James Watson Esq. of Brookhill, between Lisburn and Ballinderry, was a renowned huntsman and horseman and a local contestant at both Downpatrick and the Maze course. His last race at the Maze was on 12 October 1825 when he competed for the County Cup on a twenty-year-old favourite of his called Violet. He was at this time over sixty years old, but he was able to retire as a winner. Jockeys were used at the course but in addition 'Gentlemen' such as Watson and his brother-in-law Mr. Wakefield rode their own horses. They enjoyed local support. An engraving, after a painting presented by the Marquis of Downshire, shows Watson, dressed in his peculiar hat and hunting-coat, seated on a favourite horse 'Johnny,' on which he rode when he won a Gold Cup in a steeple chase. Grouped around the horse are several of his hounds – one of them having his head resting on his master's foot, in a stirrup.

Over the years the standing of the Maze as a social occasion reduced as it was plagued by criminal elements, both male and female. The vilest characters of both sexes attended. Personal attacks and robbery were identified with the periodical meetings and on one occasion murder, despite the efforts of the Marquis of Downshire. This occurred when a serious fight developed and the Marquis of Downshire attempted to defuse the situation by having one of the ruffians removed from the course in his own carriage. The man, a strong powerful individual, was incensed by his Lordship's action and breaking loose, jumped from the carriage and rejoined the fight, where he was stabbed to death. The visitors that used to throng the course were driven away. Where once Nobles of the land – dignitaries of the church – men of station – and the industrious population had mingled in the past, the place was condemned by the greater portion of the population. In July 1843, the Rev.

Dr. Cooke preached a sermon in Lisburn Presbyterian Church on the evils of horse racing. A public meeting later in the week denounced 'Marquisses and Earls and Baronets and Magistrates' who patronized this public nuisance.

Times change. Law and order becomes effective and horse racing is, for the public, an extremely popular pastime. The course became more accessible; the newly opened Ulster Railway Company reported that 18,503 people were carried from Belfast to Lisburn for race week. In 1921, the racing calendar over five consecutive Saturdays provided entertainment with steeplechases, hurdle races and flat races. To celebrate the Coronation in 1937 a handicap for three-year-old's was planned; the trophy valued at 50 sovereigns with 500 added.

There have been three races which had a significant impact on racing at Down Royal. The Governor's Cup was presented in 1924 by the Duke of Abercorn, who was the first Governor of Northern Ireland serving from 1922 to 1945. The Ulster Derby, named after the trophy, which was gifted by Lord Derby whose forefathers created the most famous race in the world. The first race took place in July 1936 and there were even two American entries. The third race was the Soudavar Hurdle which began in 1978. A two-day Festival of Racing, which began in 1999, became the highlight of the Northern Ireland racing calendar and played host to the first Grade 1 race of the National Hunt season in the British Isles and as such attracted many of the biggest names.

Life membership badge John Carleton 1825.
(Down Royal)

The Battle of Thermopylae, Kilwarlin

O N THE 13 JULY 1844, Thomas Osborne Davis first published the song, *A Nation Once Again* in the *Nation* newspaper and the first verse probably raised a few eyebrows at the lines, 'ancient freemen, / for Greece and Rome who bravely stood, / three hundred men and three men', and an explanation was sought in many quarters. Davis' reference to the heroic stand of Horatius and his two companions at the bridge in Rome and the last stand of the 300 Spartans at Thermopylae created an unusual link to Irish history. No more surprising perhaps, than to learn that a detailed landscaped ground plan of the Battle of Thermopylae is laid out just off a quiet country road at Kilwarlin, Co. Down. To add to our amazement we discover that this landscaped battlefield, in the grounds of a Moravian Church, is the work of a former minister, the Rev. Basil Patras Zula, from Greece.

> Kilwarlin Moravian chapel is situated in the townland of Corcreeny, on the side of a by-road. It is a neat, slated stone building, roughcast and whitewashed. It is 41 feet long and 26 feet broad in the inside. The walls are 2 feet thick. The entrance is in the west end by a passage 3 feet 6 inches wide and 13 feet long, on each side of which is a small vestry over which is a gallery looking into the body of the chapel. The pulpit is very neat. There are no pews but forms for the accommodation of 150 persons, including the gallery. The chapel was rebuilt in 1834 at the expense of the present clergyman. The old chapel was built in 1755 and was in a very ruinous state when he came there, and was seldom used except as a schoolhouse.

The Moravian Chuch at Kilwarlin

This extract, taken from the *Ordnance Survey Memoir,* July 1837, describes the church which had been rebuilt a few years previously by Basil Patras Zula, and which stands today a memorial to the eighteenth century missionary zeal of the Moravians. The history and background to the establishment of the Moravian Church at Kilwarlin is of interest, for although small in numbers their work and influence covered a wide field, and the surviving diaries and records, which they kept, provide a valuable source for local history.

The Moravian Church originated in Moravia and Bohemia from among the followers of the Czech martyr John Huss, who was burned at the stake on 6 July 1415 as a heretic. Huss could be claimed as the first 'Protestant' as it was over one hundred years later that Martin Luther posted his *Ninety-Five Theses* at Wittenberg. In 1457 a small group of his followers founded a separate Church which they called by the Latin name *Unitas Fratrum*, which in English means 'Unity of Brethren'. The Church attached importance to the role of the laity in worship, work and governance and produced the first Protestant Hymn Book in Prague in 1501, and printed and published the Kralitz Bible in 1579, which was a translation into the Czech language from the original Hebrew and Greek. They founded many schools and colleges.

In the early part of the seventeenth century the Unitas Fratrum suffered severe persecution and was almost wiped out when its churches were destroyed, services were forbidden and its followers killed and persecuted. A small group of members survived by escaping through Poland and Silesia and taking refuge in the estate of a German nobleman, Count Nicholas Ludwig von Zinzendorf. In 1727, the church was re-born and Moravian missionaries were sent to the West Indies, Greenland, South Africa and North and South America. Their arrival in England brought them into contact with John and Charles Wesley and their associates. One of these was John Cennick, who had assisted John Wesley with his work in the Bristol area, but when doctrinal differences caused the Moravians and Methodists to separate, Cennick became a minister in the Moravian Church and in 1746 he was invited to Dublin to preach.

Symbol of the Moravian Church. *'Our Lamb has conquered, let us follow Him'.*

As a result of his labours over the next few years religious societies were founded in most of the northern counties and Moravian Churches were built at Ballinderry, Gracehill and Kilwarlin. On his travels through Ireland Cennick preached at Glenavy, Ballinderry, Portmore, Magheralin, Lurgan and Moira and in August 1751 preached to large assemblies at the Maze and Magheragall, but it was a Br. Syms, in May 1752, who was first to preach at Kilwarlin. Two years later Cennick preached in the street at Lurgan to about 2,000 people and then went to Kilwarlin where half the congregation remained after his sermon until they cleared Robert Turner's land for the foundation for a new chapel, and laid the first stone. The building was completed in August 1754.

The congregation had its own resident minister but by 1813 numbers had declined and Kilwarlin was placed under the charge of the minister at Ballinderry. A period of further decline reduced the membership to six elderly people by 1834 with the church and manse in a ruinous state. The revival in the life and fortunes of the church was almost entirely due to the labours of a new minister called Basil Patras Zula, the son of a Greek chieftain and soldier. The Moravians brought an international flavour to the area but none more so than this Greek exile with his extraordinary story.

Zula was born in Greece in 1796 and he was only five years old when his father died. His mother placed him in the care of a Greek priest, hoping to fulfil his father's wishes that he would enter the church, but on reaching the age of eleven the leaders of his people insisted that he take over the chieftainship and train for military action in the War of Independence against the Ottoman Empire. He took part in the siege of Missolonghi, which was the scene of major resistance against Turkish domination. Zula turned his back on war and went to

Smyrna in Turkey where he met Sir William Eden and became his travelling companion.

Sir William and Zula visited Dublin in 1828 and stayed at a hotel in Sackville Street where it was the custom of the owner Mr. Bilton to invite his guests to take part in morning prayers. A young Moravian school teacher was introduced to Zula and she invited him to attend the Moravian Church. He was delighted to discover that she understood Greek; she had been a teacher in a Moravian boarding school in England, which included Greek in the curriculum, and through her influence he joined the church and offered himself for the ministry. After an eight month stay at the Moravian settlement at Gracehill, Co. Antrim, where he learned English, Zula returned to Dublin and married Ann Linfoot on Easter Day 1829. In 1834, Basil and Ann Zula came to serve at Kilwarlin and immediately made an impact on the local community and the dwindling congregation.

When Zula preached his first Sunday morning sermon he attracted a congregation of forty people, but one week later he had introduced an afternoon service and the church was nearly full. Two weeks later he records in his diary, "Had the pleasure to see an increase of hearers both at the morning and evening preaching." Zula went out to meet the people and was dutiful in his pastoral work. He preached in a barn belonging to a local Methodist to a large company composed mostly of Presbyterians and at Walnut Hill he preached to church members, Presbyterians, Methodists and a few Roman Catholics. He was aware that many people felt that they could not attend any place of worship because they did not have suitable clothing, so he visited them in their own homes.

Zula embarked on rebuilding the church fabric and by October 1834 an estimate had been agreed to and the following week work began on the demolition of the original structure. Its condition had so deteriorated that the timber purlins were rotted, so that when he put his foot on one while walking on the wall the whole roof fell inside the building. The workmen on the church and schoolhouse caused him problems with "some of them much given to taking whiskey", causing him to go to Belfast "to purchase slates and other materials for the building as so much drunkenness was practiced by men sent before on similar business that two or three days were idled in consequence."

The church was completed in March 1835 and soon after Zula rebuilt the manse and built a small day school. During this time Zula's position had been that of Probationer, but in January 1837 he became an ordained Minister in full charge of Kilwarlin. After his ordination the congregation presented him with a grandfather clock, which is preserved in the vestry of the church. In the vestry is a colourful watercolour drawing showing Zula in his native costume and the presence of such a distinguished and recognisable personality in the area no doubt gave rise to gossip and excited curiosity. We can imagine the reaction when he employed local labour to landscape the grounds of the church on the plan of the famous Greek Battle of Thermopylae, fought in 480 BC.

When the army of the Persian king Xerxes began its invasion of Greece the Greek force was very small, but determined to make a stand against superior numbers. Some Greek cities had united and forgotten their rivalries in their determination to oppose the Persian invasion. The Greeks chose to defend a narrow pass between the mountains and the sea called Thermopylae. A Greek force of 300 Spartans under their King Leonidas and about 6,000 soldiers from other Greek cities faced a Persian force of about 100,000. Xerxes sent out scouts who reported that in front of a wall that blocked the pass 300 Spartans were exercising. When the Persians attacked, the Greeks fought off wave after wave. The Spartans pretended to retreat so that the Persians chased them, then they would turn and in the confusion, kill many of the enemy. After two days of battle a Greek traitor approached the Persian king with information that would allow the Persian army to move secretly through the mountains and surround the Greeks, in front and behind. The Greeks had been betrayed; Leonidas chose to fight to the end. He told the Greek soldiers to flee, but his Spartan force would fight on. They fought to the death.

Bishop J.H. Foy explains how this strange battlefield in a garden was constructed in a circular 'hollow' formed by the Church driveway.

Basil Patras Zula in native costume.
(FGW)

Six stone steps leading down into the hollow represent the eastern entrance to Thermopylae. Opposite them, near the entrance gates, is a grassy hillock, the Mount Acta of the original battlefield. To the right of the Church driveway, as seen from the manse entrance, is a small ornamental lake representing the Aegean Sea and from this lake an underground stream, representing the hot springs, which gave Thermopylae its name, runs through the hollow. On the left of the hollow is a grassy slope representing the foothills of the Callidromon range of mountains through which the Pass of Thermopylae ran and beyond it a loftier mound, which represents Mount Callidromos. Between the lower and loftier mounds is a narrow defile representing the secret pass revealed by the Greek traitor. In the middle of the hollow is a small ornamental pond around which were originally twenty-four flower beds each in the shape of the Greek alphabet.

Only two flower beds remain – Alpha and Omega. Zula is said to have retained an irrational fear of the Turks and lived in fear of attack to the extent that the Kilwarlin manse incorporated several emergency escape measures. All the downstairs rooms had two doors, there were two separate staircases and a room at the rear built on stilts had a trap-door, which led to a hiding place under the floor. There were no Turkish reprisals, no need for escape, but in the manner of his death Basil Patras Zula has a place in the folklore of the district. The account is given here because it has become folklore without any support from surviving records, and is completely at variance to the *Fraternal Messenger* report published in 1850 during Ann Zula's lifetime.

The story goes that Zula was seen one day on the road near the Manse engaged in earnest conversation with strangers of foreign appearance and that shortly afterwards he made an unexplained journey to Dublin leaving his wife behind. News was received from Dublin some days later that he had died suddenly. Those who accompanied the coffin back to Kilwarlin were surprised by its great weight and to satisfy their curiosity they opened the lid to discover that it was full of stones. They said nothing and it was buried in the normal manner.

Zula died of fever in Dublin on 4 October 1844 and four days later he was laid to rest in the burial ground beside Kilwarlin church. His widow Ann lived on in the manse and conducted a boarding school for select young ladies in a wing of the building, which she had constructed for the purpose. She died in 1858, aged sixty-five, and is buried alongside her husband.

Marquis of Downshire Memorial, Hillsborough

IN THE MONUMENT FIELD on the Dromore side of Hillsborough stands a tall fluted Greek Doric column on a square podium and stylobate possibly 130 feet high with a more than life size statue atop. This column was erected as a memorial to the third Marquis of Downshire (1788–1845), who died in Blesssington, Co. Wicklow. Inset in the base on the north face are the Downshire arms with the family motto – *Per Deum et Ferrum Obtinui* – "By God and the sword I obtained possession" – a neat description of how the Hills obtained over 100,000 acres, mainly in Co. Down, and eventually became one of the largest land-owning families in the country. It has this inscription:

> To commemorate the public and private virtues of the most Honorable Arthur Wills Blundell Sandys Trumbull Hill, Third Marquis of Downshire, Lieutenant of the County of Down, Colonel of the Royal South Down Regiment of Militia and Knight of the Most Illustrious Order of St Patrick. Alike distinguished for patriotism, rectitude of principle, of honesty, of purpose upholding his station with becoming dignity, he was also mindful of the wants of others and practised its duties with benevolence and humility which won the regard of every virtuous mind, adding lustre to his exalted rank. Those who best knew his worth and admired the uprightness of his character and conduct in the several relations of life, have erected this Monumental Column as a token of their friendship and esteem, 1848.

Above and below: Memorial to the 3rd Marquis of Downshire. *(JSH)*

The third Marquis died in April 1845, during an inspection on horseback of one of the townlands on his Blessington estate. According to a newspaper report, the agent, William Owen, who escorted him, had ridden on ahead to inform one of the tenants that the landlord wished to speak with him. Looking back, Owen saw the Marquis prostrate on the ground, the mare walking over him; he hastened to help, but his Lordship had expired. The inquest jury's verdict found that his Lordship had 'died by the visitation of God.' The return of his remains to the family vault in Hillsborough was said to have resulted in the longest funeral procession ever seen in Ireland. He was highly respected by all his tenants. On his coming of age, he had taken upon himself, as a matter of honour, the payment of the remaining debts of his father and grandfather and he had implemented sweeping reforms in the management of the estates whilst maintaining fairness to tenants.

Arthur Trumbull Hill on horseback.
(Equine Sketches, courtesy of the National Portrait Gallery)

Funeral of the Third Marquis of Downshire at Hillsborough Parish Church.
(Illustrated London News, April 1845)

The funeral from Dublin to Hillsborough took place some days later and was accompanied by the more notable Blessington tenants. The attendance and progress of the funeral train was a measure of the regard in which the deceased nobleman was universally held. The mourning coaches, which held the Marquis of Downshire, Baron Sandys, Lord George Hill, J.T. Reilly, Esq., T. Crosier, Esq. and H. Murray, Esq., were accompanied by a number of private carriages, and followed by a procession of gentlemen dressed in black, with crepe on the left arm.

On Tuesday evening, the cortege reached Newry, attended by a large body of townspeople, and the coffin was deposited for the night in St Mary's Church, the vicar having read the funeral service. On Wednesday morning, the funeral bell announced the re-assembling of the train. The procession had just left Newry, when it was joined by parties of mounted tenantry from Hilltown, Rathfriland, and adjacent places. About six miles from the town more tenants from the Fortescue estate fell into the ranks. Constantly increasing in this manner, the cortege approached Loughbrickland and Banbridge. About two hundred inhabitants of Banbridge assembled at the Downshire Arms, and proceeded, two and two, attired in black, to meet the funeral train at Loughbrickland. They formed a line on each side of the road till the procession passed on, when they took their place in the rear. At Banbridge the hearse and mourning carriages halted for about an hour and a half, and then set forward, followed by the rest of the procession. At Dromore the inhabitants closed their shops, and vast numbers of them joined in. The cathedral bell solemnly pealed out and on the tower the Union flag flew reversed.

About two miles from Dromore, the procession was met by the tenantry of Hillsborough and its vicinity; and, from one to two miles, the highway was filled with a dense living mass, numbering from 3,000 to 4,000, in carriages and on horseback and on foot. When Hillsborough was reached the coffin was deposited in the Castle. Next morning, multitudes from Belfast, Lisburn, and other towns, arrived long before the hour appointed for the burial service and the body lay in state at the Castle. The outside coffin was of very strong oak, covered with fine crimson silk velvet, finished with gilt nails, massive gilt handles and escutcheons, and a large inscription-plate, with the family arms, surmounted by the coronet and crest. The inner coffin was of mahogany, lined with white silk, padded, and highly polished. This was enclosed in a strong leaden coffin.

After the ceremonial had been witnessed by thousands, the tenantry, in their scarfs and hatbands, were drawn up on each side of the streets leading from the Castle to the Church, and at one o'clock the procession began to move from the Castle. On arriving at the door of the Church, the procession was met by the Rev. Mr. Mesham, domestic chaplain of the Marquis of Downshire, who read the service for the burial of the dead and afterwards delivered a funeral address from Revelation, chapter 14, verse 13. The sermon being ended, the funeral train left the church and proceeded to the adjoining family vault.

Fourth Marquis of Downshire

Standing on a high stone plinth in a small park opposite the gates to the Parish Church of St Malachy, Hillsborough, is a large bronze statue of Arthur Wills Blundell Sandys Trumbull Windsor, Fourth Marquis of Downshire, who was popularly known as the 'Big Marquis'. He was born on 6 August 1812 and died at Herne Bay on 6 August 1868. Portrayed more than life-size in gum boots and sporting a black-thorn stick in one hand, with an enormous shawl over his other arm, the statue, erected by friends and tenants, and modelled in 1873, is the work of Samuel Ferres Lynn and was cast by Prince & Co. of Southwark. We are familiar with Lynn's work from his statue of Dr Henry Cooke, 'The Black Man', with his back to 'Inst' and the figure of the Prince Consort on the Albert Memorial clock tower.

The dinner given in 1833 for the Earl of Hillsborough when he came of age was, perhaps, one of the largest gatherings of stalwart yeomanry in Co. Down. The following year he was High Sheriff of Down and took the chair at the great mass meeting of Protestants held on the outskirts of Hillsborough on 30 October 1834, when Dr Henry Cooke proclaimed the banns of marriage between Episcopacy and Presbyterianism. In October 1867, on the anniversary of the Protestant Demonstration of 1834, he presided over a second Hillsborough demonstration called to protest against any interference with

Right: Early postcard of the monument to the Fourth Marquis of Downshire, 1906.

Far right: The Fourth Marquis of Downshire.

ecclesiastical endowments in Ireland. His reaction to the Irish potato famine of 1846–47 was one of action. He remained in the country when many of the upper class were leaving and implemented relief schemes that cost him more than £20,000. The following spring, week after week, he visited the less independent section of his tenants and distributed many thousands of pounds to them. At a public meeting, called to arrange for relief in the distress caused by the potato famine, he stated that he would stand by his people and attend to their wants should he be obliged to pledge the last acre of his property for that purpose.

The Fourth Marquis, like his father, supported the steps being taken to promote the revival of the Irish language and when he inherited the title he was greeted by the tenantry from Hillsborough with banners inscribed *Céad Mile Fáilte*. A Gaelic society called *Cuideacht Gaeilge Uladh* or Ulster Gaelic Society had been founded in Belfast in 1830 under the presidency of the Third Marquis of Downshire, with Dr Bryce, the eventual headmaster of the Belfast Academical Institution, and Robert McAdam, who established the Soho Foundry in Belfast, as secretaries. The aims of the society were to gather manuscripts, to employ a teacher of the living language, and to publish books. The first publication of the Ulster Gaelic Society was an Irish translation of Maria Edgeworth's works *Forgive and Forget* and *Rosanna*. The book contained the following dedication to Lord Downshire.

My Lord,

Permit us in the name of the Ulster Gaelic Society, to inscribe this little work to your Lordship, as a sincere but inadequate token of their respect for the patriotic interest you have taken in the resuscitation of our long lost national literature. Actuated by that zeal, which you have always shown for the promotion of education, your Lordship no sooner heard of the existence of our society, than you came forward without solicitation, and added your name to the list of its members. …

We hope that the tales that have been fixed upon will be thought not unsuitable to the peculiar state of Ireland, and we know your Lordship will join us in wishing that the humblest of our countrymen may attain the independence and comfort which rewarded the industry of the farmer of "Rosanna" and that men of all parties, laying aside their animosities, may learn to "Forgive and Forget".

> We have the honour to be,
> My Lord,
> Your Lordship's most obedient servants.
> E.J. Bryce, R.S. McAdam Secretaries

Regium Donum

O N A PERIMETER WALL of Hillsborough Fort, just to the left of the main gate, a weathered stone plaque is built into the wall. The plaque, which is a little worn in places, carries the following inscription:

> 6 feet south east of this slab the Regium Donum was signed by King William III of glorious memory to the Presbyterian body which they were deprived of by PM Gladstone in 1869.

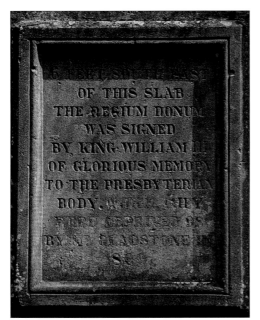

The Regium Donum plaque. *(GG)*

An endowment, which became known afterwards under the name of the Regium Donum, or Royal Gift, was first granted by Charles II, a man thought unlikely to favour Presbyterianism. Sir Arthur Forbes, a friend of the Church, was in London in 1672 and met with the King; one positive outcome was a proposed grant of £1,200 per annum. The grant was reduced to £600, the amount available when the state of the Treasury became known. This was the origin of the endowment which the Irish Presbyterian Church enjoyed from this time onward, except for some periods when payment lapsed, until the passing of the Irish Church Act in 1869.

King William III landed from the yacht *Mary* at Carrickfergus on Saturday 14 June 1690. He travelled to Belfast and stayed there for five nights and was visited at the castle by a delegation of Presbyterian ministers, led by Rev. Patrick Adair, minister of Belfast, Rev. Archibald Hamilton, Armagh, and Rev. William Adair, Ballyeaston, who presented him with a loyal address of welcome. On Thursday, the King left Belfast and proceeded to Hillsborough where he issued an order to Christopher Carleton, Collector of Customs at Belfast, authorising him to make a payment of £1,200 per annum, the Regium Donum, to the clergy of the Presbyterian Church, having been assured 'of their constant labour to unite the hearts of others in zeal and loyalty towards us.' The previous payment of £600 had been paid irregularly and then stopped altogether. The minister from the First Presbyterian Church in Lisburn was one of the churchmen selected to be in the deputation to meet with the King at Hillsborough.

During the reign of Queen Anne, the Bishops protested about the Regium Donum and the government was urged to remove it from them, which was actually done before the close of the reign. Under George III, the Regium Donum was increased by adding £1,000 per annum in 1784, and a further £5,000 per annum in 1792. The Seceders, who received no State support in the past, were granted £500 per annum due to the influence of the Earl of Hillsborough, and they also shared in the 1792 increase of £5,000. The Regium Donum was increased by a very large amount in 1803 and the method of distribution revised.

Up until that time each minister had received £32 per annum from this source. Now the 186 congregations of the Synod of Ulster and the Presbytery of Antrim were divided into three classes, containing sixty-two each, the classification being made according to the size and importance of the congregations. The largest congregations were put in the first class and their ministers were to receive £100 per annum, those in the second class £75 per annum and those of the third £50, all Irish currency. The Synod objected to the system of classification, but their objections were overruled. The Seceders did not share in the increase and pressed for an augmented endowment. In 1809 that request was granted, but their ministers were paid on a lower scale, the three classes receiving £70, £50 and £40 per congregation per annum. In 1838, the principle of classification was done away with. In that year the Regium Donum was equalized and each minister, both of the Synod of Ulster and the Secession Synod, received £75 per annum, Irish. The level of endowment continued at this figure until it was abolished by the Irish Church Act.

We return to the plaque quoted at the beginning of this article and the reference to Prime Minister Gladstone. In the general election of 1868 the Liberal party secured a comfortable victory which paved the way for the introduction of Gladstone's Irish Church Bill on 1 March 1869. Despite opposition, the Bill received the Royal Assent in July. The Irish Church Act disestablished the Church of Ireland and deprived the Presbyterian Church of the endowment it had enjoyed for almost two centuries. The Act allowed all recipients of the Regium Donum either to continue to draw it during their life, or to commute it for a lump sum to be paid at once and it was permissible that this commutation might be effected by each individual minister in his own personal interest, had the Church so decided. A special meeting of the General Assembly was called in January 1870 to consider the position. After four days of debate and with only five dissenting voices the General Assembly elected to commute their 'Bounty' as an endowment fund, and the sum of £587,735 was placed in the Church treasury, from which current and future ministers would receive an annual stipend. Today, Presbyterian ministers still receive an amount from the Regium Donum fund. (What would that be worth today? A simple Purchasing Power Calculator would say the relative value is £51,610,000. This answer is obtained by multiplying £587,735 by the percentage increase in the RPI from 1870 to 2016.)

By 1870, these important questions of income and finance, issues of crisis proportions, had been put to bed and the Church was able to focus on another question which was a cause for debate for over two decades – the lawfulness of the use of instrumental music in public worship.

Ardens Sed Virens

The burning bush with the Latin inscription *Ardens sed virens* – "Burning but flourishing" – is the recognised symbol in Irish Presbyterian Churches. The symbol is taken from Exodus 3:2 and the earliest use of a burning bush was in the first edition of the Presbyterian newspaper *The Banner of Ulster,* published on 10 June 1842. Edited by the Rev. William

Banner of Ulster
masthead

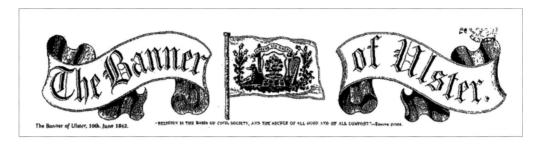

Gibson, it was published twice weekly. Back then, it featured a burning bush with an open Bible beneath it and on either side an Irish wolfhound and an Irish harp. A shamrock and thistle were intertwined against the background of an Irish round tower. All emblems of an Irish identity were eventually removed leaving the familiar burning bush and inscription.

'Religion is the basis of civil society, and the source of all good and of all comfort'.

Edmund Burke

Sir Hamilton Harty

Sir Hamilton Harty.
(Classic FM)

Herbert Hamilton Harty was born in Hillsborough, Co. Down, on 4 December 1879. His father, William Michael Harty (1852–1918), was organist in St Malachy's, the local Church of Ireland. His mother, Annie Elizabeth, was the daughter of Joseph Hamilton Richards, a soldier from Bray, Co. Wicklow. Under the patronage of the Marquis of Downshire the family were provided with an official residence in Ballynahinch Street.

Harty's father taught him the viola, piano and counterpoint, and at the age of 12, he followed his father's profession and was appointed organist at Magheragall Church, Co. Antrim. In Hillsborough, they both played the large Snetzler organ, which may be seen in the west gallery of the church.

Harty took further posts in his teenage years as organist in St Barnabas' Church, Belfast, and choirmaster and organist at Christ Church, Bray. While at the latter, he came under the influence of Michele Esposito (1855–1929), professor of piano at the Royal Irish Academy of Music, with whom he developed a lifelong friendship. Later he described the Italian as the presiding genius of all that was music in Ireland 'as an all-round musician, unsurpassed in Europe. I send him for criticism everything I write; and put as explicit faith in him now as when a boy – he has always been right.' Harty concentrated on studying the piano and developed a reputation in the art of pianoforté accompaniment.

Harty moved to London when aged about twenty, soon becoming a well-known piano accompanist. Among those that he accompanied in his early days was the soprano, Agnes Nicholls, whom he married on 15 July 1904. The marriage did not last. In the same year Harty made his debut as a conductor at the *Feis Ceoil* music festival in Dublin, with the first performance of his *Irish Symphony*. For the Cardiff Festival of 1907 the solo part of his setting of Keats' *Ode to a Nightingale* was undertaken by his wife. As a composer, he was almost entirely self-taught, intuitive and wrote throughout his career; many of his works were well received. During the first decade of the century he published some of his best-known songs: *Sea-Wrack* and *Three Traditional Ulster Airs, The Blue Hills of Antrim, My Lagan Love*, and *Black Sheela of the Silver Eye,* 1905; *Lane o' the Thrushes,* 1907 and *Six Songs of Ireland,* 1908.

In his career as a conductor Harty was particularly noted as an interpreter of the music of Berlioz. From 1920 to 1933 he was the chief conductor of the Hallé Orchestra in Manchester, which he returned to the high standards and critical acclaim that it had

The Harty house, Ballynahinch Street.

enjoyed under its founder, Charles Hallé. His last permanent post was with the London Symphony Orchestra (LSO), but it lasted only two years, from 1932 to 1934. During his career Harty made many recordings and travelled to America and Australia. Shortly after his departure from the LSO, Harty began to suffer the symptoms of a brain tumour. After surgery, he resumed his career. In March 1939, in the Queen's Hall he conducted the first performance of his *Children of Lir* in front of a capacity audience. The *Manchester Guardian* records the occasion:

Gold Medal of the Royal Philharmonic Society.

He at once lifted the occasion far above sentiment and goodwill by conducting with simple mastery a magnificent performance of a new work of his own and one of the most poetic compositions of any British composer of the last decade or two. His poem for orchestra, The *Children of Lir*, is an act of courage … Sir Hamilton trusts to the traditional stuff of his art … he has given us a work which appeals to the heart and moves us with beauty of tone and beauty of conception.

He had engagements with the Liverpool Philharmonic and several with the BBC. He conducted for the last time with the BBC Symphony Orchestra at Tunbridge Wells on 1 December 1940. He died two months later at the age of 61. A plaque was erected at 33 Brunswick Square, Hove, by the Regency Society of Brighton and Hove, to mark the house where he died. It was unveiled by David Greer, the Hamilton Harty Professor of Music at Queen's University, Belfast.

Hamilton Harty was knighted in 1925 and received the Mus. Doc. of Dublin University in the same year. In 1933, he was given the degree of Doctor of Laws by Queen's University, Belfast, and in 1934 he was awarded the Gold Medal of the Royal Philharmonic Society. Sir Hamilton Harty always had a great confidence in the future of British music. Of swing music, he had this to say – 'Jazz is a blight. It is sensual, noisy and incredibly stupid'.

Bird bath, designed by Rosamund Praeger, marks the burial place of the composer's ashes in the grounds of Hillsborough Parish Church.
(JSH)

The Lagan Navigation

I N 1637, SIR GEORGE Rawdon suggested digging a canal from the River Lagan at Moira to Lough Neagh, a distance of six miles over fairly level country. Nothing happened until 1753 when a petition in favour of a waterway was made to the Irish House of Commons by:

> ... the sovereigns and burgesses of Belfast and Hillsborough, the inhabitants of Lisburn and the seneschals and grand juries of the manors of Killultagh and Moira.

An Act was obtained on 24 October 1753 'for making the River Lagan navigable, and opening a passage by water between Lough Neagh and the town of Belfast in the County of Antrim'. The River Lagan was to be made navigable as far as Lisburn by building locks and straightening the course of the river. In 1756 the following notice appeared in the *Belfast News Letter*.

> Alexander McClure in Belenoghan and Thomas Knox near Banbridge hath begun the canal near Drumbridge and want labourers. All good labourers may expect good usage and nine pence per day and their pay once a week.

Under the direction of a canal engineer of Dutch ancestry, called Thomas Omer, the section to Lisburn was completed at a cost of £70,000 by September 1763. Between 1763 and 1765 the river was made navigable from Lisburn up to Sprucefield, but nothing further was done for many years. The Corporation responsible for carrying on the inland

The Lagan near Lisburn.
(FGW)

navigation was operating on a restricted financial basis. Provisions were made in the Act of 1753 to raise funds, in the eleven-year period covered by the legislation, from the area that the canal would pass through by an additional duty of one penny per gallon on ale and four pence per gallon on spirits … within that part of the district of Lisburn commonly known and distinguished by the gaugers' walks of Belfast, Lisburn, Moira and Hillsborough.

The *Belfast News Letter* provided readers with a report of the opening event.

(FGW)

> The *Lord Hertford,* a lighter capable of carrying fifty tons, made the first voyage on the new canal. Mr James Craig, the owner, had invited a party to make the trip and to dine as his guests on board. Food of all descriptions was provided and twelve varieties of wine were served. As the boat sailed along past bleach greens and fields where corn was being cut, a band aboard played popular airs. Hundreds of people stood on the banks of the river and some walked along the tow-path through Lambeg and Hilden as far as Lisburn. In the town that evening the windows of many houses were brightly illuminated and bonfires blazed in the market place. Lord Hertford had instructed his agent to supply barrels of ale for those of the townspeople who wished to drink his health. Dancing and merrymaking to the tunes of more than fifty fiddlers went on till the early hours of the morning.

The canal had operational problems from the outset, as a letter addressed to Lord Downshire by John Williamson of Lambeg and dated 10 February 1765 clearly indicates:

> A large fleet of colliers arrived lately into the port of Belfast, and people prepared to get great quantities of the coal up by the new navigation. Three boats were loaded with from ten to fifteen tons each, and they set off in fine weather, but a heavy shower coming on they were stopped. They were five weeks and two days on their voyage, and were liked to have been all wrecked in a flood. Before they got back to Belfast for a second cargo the cars had carried away all the coals.

Omer had difficulty funding further engineering work, both above and below Lisburn, and it was apparent that there were serious problems in using the course of the river for navigation due to severe winter flooding. Various proposals were put forward to abandon the river course for commercial navigation and to construct an entirely new canal separate from the river. Thirty years were to pass before a very imperfect Lagan Navigation system reached Lough Neagh.

Fast forward to the present day and an ambitious £100 million plus plan from the Lagan Navigation Trust to see the Lagan Navigation from Belfast Harbour to Lough Neagh re-opened and developed to make a significant contribution to the Northern Ireland economy, presumably without draining the said economy. Some would say difficult to achieve – the Belfast to Lisburn stretch of the canal was never a success and the section from Sprucefield to Moira has been overlaid by the M1 Motorway. The Trust operates from the appropriately named Navigation House.

Navigation House

NAVIGATION HOUSE IS SITUATED on the Hillsborough Road at Sprucefield and is set in a secluded mature landscaped garden, which leads from a small gated entrance screen via a narrow driveway. Once the home of the manager of the Lagan Navigation Canal, in the days when coal lighters plied the canal from Belfast to Lough Neagh, it is in the process of being restored. This historic home, which was built in 1866, will be the new headquarters of the Lagan Navigation Trust.

A Victorian house in red brick with sliding sash windows and yellow brick trims, it has a portico style door surround with tall narrow sidelights flanked with columns on each side and stone steps at its entrance. Its roof is of natural slate with exposed rafters. The building is located close by the Union Locks, which are protected as a scheduled monument, and near to a listed former lock keeper's cottage. The Trust has found the perfect headquarters.

Navigation House
(JSH)

Union Locks

THE UNION LOCKS ARE situated to the rear of the garden of Navigation House and can be approached by a short walk from Blaris Road. Between 1763 and 1765 the Lagan was made navigable up to what became the site of the Union Locks at Sprucefield. These locks were the termination of the Lagan Navigation for over thirty years. The remains of the Union Locks (Locks No 14, 15, 16 and 17) consist of a flight of four locks with an intermediate basin by which barges could reach the long summit level from the river. Here the canal finally parted with the river, the locks raised the barges some twenty-six feet over a distance of one hundred yards. The canal from here ran almost due west through Co. Down before turning north-west to cross the Lagan over an aqueduct near Spencer's Bridge, on past Soldierstown, entering Friar's Glen and the Broadwater, then on to Aghalee and the descent to Lough Neagh at Ellis' Gut. A steam tug was maintained at Ellis' Gut to tow barges across the lough.

The new canal had a surface width of 56 ft. and was 7 ft. deep. Above the Union Locks it had a summit level eleven miles long, followed by a descent to Lough Neagh made over ten locks in just under four miles. It was officially opened on 1 January 1794. The officials assembled at Hillsborough on New Year's Eve and having breakfasted the next morning at the home of the engineer, Richard Owen at Sion Mill, near the aqueduct, they embarked from there at ten o'clock and reached the Lough about sunset, arriving at Port Chichester, as they attempted to call Ellis' Gut in honour of the Donegall family. The final section of the Lagan Navigation cost £62,000 and was built entirely at the expense of the Marquis

The dilapidated Union Locks. *(JSH)*

of Donegall. The completed canal was not a success. A story current at the time stated that a ship had sailed to the West Indies and back to Belfast by the time a lighter had journeyed from Belfast to Lough Neagh. In 1809 and 1843 further improvements were carried out. The dawning of the twentieth century saw a further decline in the importance of the canal in face of increasing competition from road and rail.

From 1947 there was no traffic on the canal beyond Lisburn and the Ministry of Commerce announced that all the canals in Northern Ireland would close in the spring of 1954. The Inland Navigation Act (NI) was passed in April 1954 and later that year the Coalisland Canal, the Upper Bann Navigation and the Lagan Canal above Lisburn were closed. Below Lisburn, on the Belfast side, the canal remained open for another four years, but was closed on 1 July 1958.

Ballyskeagh High Bridge

ONE OF THE IMPRESSIVE sights encountered on a journey along the tow-path is that of Ballyskeagh High Bridge. Philip Dixon Hardy (1793–1875), in his *Twenty-one views in Belfast and its Neighbourhood* calls it the 'Forth Bridge' by which he meant the 'Fourth' bridge. The first bridge was at Newforge, the second at Shaw's Bridge and the third at Drumbeg, making this one the fourth. Fred Hamond has stated, 'historically it is of interest on account of its mid-eighteenth century construction date, architecturally, it is arguably the most impressive canal bridge, in terms of scale and proportion, to survive in the Province. Finally, it makes a very significant impact on the landscape hereabouts.' The bridge carries the road from Lambeg to Drumbeg on an S-bend over a deep cut for the canal just above the eighth lock. The canal and tow-path are spanned by arches, one broad and one narrow, built in reddish sandstone rubble with cut stone voussoirs. Wear marks from the barge tow-ropes are visible on the central pier, which also carries a benchmark. It is said that the last person to be hanged for sheep stealing was executed at Ballyskeagh Bridge. It was a public execution and those who attended were asked if they had any messages for their friends in Hell, as the condemned man could pass them on when he arrived there.

Ballyskeagh High Bridge, 2007.
(FGW)

Far left: Sketch by W.W. Legge, 1816
(ILC & LM)

Left: The 'Forth Bridge', Ballyskeagh.

The Lock Keeper's House

Ballyskeagh steps.
(FGW)

To the side of Ballyskeagh High Bridge a flight of thirty-seven steps leads to the lock keeper's house, which was built by Thomas Omer, the canal engineer, between 1759 and 1763. The attractive two-storey stone building, in Omer's individual style, is similar to the lock keeper's house at Drum Bridge. The house, which was restored by 'Hearth' in 1992–93, is described in the *Archaeological Survey of County Down* as:

…square in plan and of two floors, built of rubble with wrought dressings; the roof is slated … at the centre of each elevation is a recess, with semi-circular arched head with key-block, rising from the platband; on the N, the recess contains a door with block architrave and square head formed of stepped and projecting voussoirs, the keystone rising to the level of the platband which is continuous across the recess; the recesses on the other elevations contain windows.

The house originally afforded good views in each direction, which allowed the lock keeper enough time to attend to his lock when barges came into view. A report of 1884 suggested that this was a job for the younger man when William Ward at Ballyskeagh changed places with his son Arthur, who operated the Mossvale lock. The reason given was 'the heavier duties and long climb up to the lock-house at Ballyskeagh were becoming too

Lock keeper's house, Ballyskeagh.
(FGW)

much for an old man.' The duties of the lock keepers were laid down in the Lagan Navigation Company Regulations, which stated that they were responsible for watching over the banks, towing paths, locks, weirs, overflows, waste sluices, bridges and quays, and keeping in repair the banks and roads under their charge. Rules governing the operation and maintenance of the locks included the lock keeper sounding his horn when a loaded lighter entered his lock, and in periods of dry weather keeping his lock gate properly secured with moss to prevent the waste of water. The lock-house was bought in 1955 by a retired lock keeper, William McCue and following his death it lay empty, was vandalised, and sat as a burnt-out shell for about fifteen years. Following its restoration, Hearth was presented in 1998 with an Award of Merit from the Historic Buildings Council for Northern Ireland.

Chrome Hill

The Niven coat of arms.
(FGW)

CHROME HILL, A SECLUDED house of great character, sits on the Co. Down side of the River Lagan at Wolfenden's Bridge. The original small farm dwelling, out of which the house has grown, was probably built some time in the second half of the seventeenth century and Abraham Wolfenden, who gave shelter here to King William on his way to the Boyne in 1690, is the earliest known occupant. The house was at various times called Harmony Hill and Lambeg House. Sir Charles Brett writes:

> …the present exterior appearance, a five-bay two-storey white-painted roughcast house with lower extension on the right and taller extension to the left, is mostly of the early 1830s, when Richard Niven bought the Lambeg works… he changed the name of the house, formerly known as Lambeg House, to Chrome Hill.

A copy of Benn's, *The History of the Town of Belfast,* which is inscribed Richard Niven, Chrome Hill, 15 Aug. 1823, would indicate an earlier date for him being in residence. Samuel Lewis in his *Topographical Dictionary*, 1837, writes:

> Chrome Hill, also a spacious modern mansion, was erected by R. Niven Esq., late of Manchester, who established here some extensive works for printing muslin, in which he first applied with success his invention of the 'Ba Chrome', now universally used… from which circumstance he named his estate.

Richard Niven inserted his own coat of arms into the pediment above the front door when he bought the house and carried out some alterations and improvements. The present entrance and the driveway, which leads in a semi-circular sweep up to the front door, was formed by Niven before the 1860s. This gave visitors the best view of the west front of the house on their approach. Originally the old drive, which was reputed to be the old road from Belfast, started at Ballyskeagh High Bridge, ran past the stable yard, along in front of the house, and finally came down to the river at the bridge. This last section from the house to the river was made redundant and has now

Chrome Hill
(FGW)

Richard Niven Jnr.
(ILC & LM)

disappeared. The driveway from the canal bridge survived into the twentieth century but by that time the gate lodge had disappeared and part of the gates was all that remained. There is a secondary entrance, a steep driveway up to the stable yard and the back of the house from the road directly opposite the factory entrance to Lambeg Mills. Niven's new entrance gates and the entrance opposite the factory, with its original eighteenth-century gates and piers, are in use today.

Richard Niven died in 1866, and is buried in the parish churchyard in a grave surrounded by an iron railing. His son, Richard Niven Jnr. (1839–1914), formerly of Chrome Hill, and afterwards of Marlborough Park, Belfast, died at Brighton in 1914. A member of the firm of Richardson & Niven, linen manufacturers, he was a man of taste and culture; an amateur artist in both watercolour and oil, with an abiding interest in literature. An enthusiastic Orangeman and historian, his publications varied from *Orangeism as it was and is; A concise history of the rise and progress of the Institution*, to the light hearted and humorous volumes; *On the road to the Boyne* and *The life of St Patrick*. His widowed mother continued to live in the house until her death in 1899. It then went through a succession of owners and was purchased in 1924 by the Downer family. Mrs Margaret Josephine Downer lived there until her death in 1967, when Robert McKinstry the architect acquired it. In 2004 the house was purchased by its present owner, Dawson Stelfox, also an architect and the first Irishman to conquer Everest.

Below: The Wesley Tree. *(FGW)*

Far right: Bust of John Wesley (1703–1791), Staffordshire Pottery 1784, by Enoch Wood. *(ILC & LM)*

The Wesley Tree

THE GARDENS OF CHROME Hill house contain some fine trees. To the left of the entrance drive stands a beech, known as the Wesley tree, which was planted by John Wesley, the founder of Methodism, who visited Lisburn on a number of occasions. In 1787, he visited Lambeg House, at that time the home of Richard Wolfenden. During his stay here, John Wesley is said to have intertwined two beech saplings and to have done so to demonstrate the union of the Methodist people and the Church of Ireland. The two beech trees have grown together as one and are known as the Wesley Tree. Close to this historic site a covenant was formally signed on 26 September 2002 committing the Methodist Church in Ireland and the Church of Ireland to a common and fuller relationship. The Church of Ireland Primate, Archbishop Robin Eames, and W. Winston Graham, President of the Methodist Church in Ireland, signed the commitment following a simple act of worship.

Lisburn's Industrial Past

In the past, the town of Lisburn and its neighbourhood was fortunate in possessing families who fostered, developed and expanded several industries that made its name synonymous with linen. Weaving, bleaching, linen yarn spinning and thread making were the chief sources of the town's growth and prosperity, which is celebrated today with the designation Irish Linen Centre. Some of the town's major industrial greats are enshrined in the following verse:

> Here sits industry laurel-crowned,
> With capital and labour meeting,
> In union on one common ground,
> Within the world's great marts competing;
> Where Coulson's damask, Barbour's thread,
> With Stewart's and the The Island Spinning,
> In workmanship the world have led
> High honours from the nations winning.

Coulsons of Lisburn

A grave in the Cathedral graveyard, which has recently been restored, is that of the Coulson family. William Coulson (1739–1801) established a damask manufactory in Lisburn in 1764. By 1766 it had moved to larger premises where the library now stands in Linenhall Street. It was a long single-storey thatched building. The company was renowned for its fine linens and elaborately designed and woven patterns. When Coulson commenced trading, the looms and patterns were primitive, but before long improvements were made by means of the Draw-loom, so called because the threads arranged for forming the pattern were raised by young assistants called draw-boys. This branch of the linen business reached an unrivalled level of perfection. By the early nineteenth century William's four sons, John, William, Walter and James developed the firm until it achieved fame and distinction. William Coulson enjoyed a large share of Court favour, having successfully worked armorial devices, national emblems and heraldic designs into the fabric. The recognition of his success by British royalty added largely to his fame. The firm of Coulson was honoured by receiving a Patent

Coulson's Damask
Manufactory
(ILC & LM)

Royal Warrant, 1811

or Royal Warrant, dated July 10, 1811, from His Royal Highness, the Prince of Wales (the Prince Regent). It was in the names of J. W. & W. Coulson, John, William and Walter. It was said to be the first issued by the Royal Family. The Rev John Dubourdieu wrote in 1812:

In the manufactory there are about fifty looms employed for damask which require about two hundred hands, but the establishment alone employs, in and out of the factory, about two hundred and fifty looms, giving employment to about five hundred hands.

Henry Bayly paid tribute to:

…the kindness and care shown by the Messrs Coulson for the welfare and happiness of those in their employ. To those who have grown old in their service, a free house is granted and a small weekly pension allowed.

Coulsons were slow to adopt the invention of Joseph Marie Jacquard (1752–1834), which replaced the need for the draw-boys in case this led to unemployment of their workers.

Between the years 1834–1837 there was a family dispute and the factory was divided into two by the introduction of a simple wall and two firms were created – William Coulson & Sons and James Coulson & Co. Hill Crothers was the chief designer of the latter firm. One of the social events of the London season was the Waterloo Banquet at Apsley House. The Duke's annual celebration of the anniversary was particularly memorable in 1838, the year of Queen Victoria's Coronation. In some of the cloths that were made for the Royal Household a centrepiece bearing the word 'Waterloo' was interwoven into them. Up to 1938 these cloths were still in use for the dinner which was held on the eve of the anniversary of the battle. James Coulson continued to receive a large share of the orders for the Royal Household. He also received appointments from the Vice-Regal office at Dublin Castle, Czar Alexander II of Russia, George I, King of the Hellenes, Leopold, Duke of Tuscany and the gentry both at home and abroad.

At the Great Exhibition in 1851, Mr James Coulson received a diploma and a gold medal. He died later that year, aged 76, and left his business to Mr James Ward, Strawberry Hill, Lisburn. He was succeeded by his son, Captain W.T. Ward, who held a commission in the London Irish Rifles. Captain Ward sold the business to Messrs Hampton and Sons Ltd., London, who carried on the work in Lisburn through a difficult period up to 1931 when it closed down. The looms were broken up and the patterns sold for scrap. William Coulson carried on in business until 1968.

William Barbour and Sons

Hilden Flax Mills
(Marcus Ward & Co., Belfast)

Hilden Mill's once impressive outline, its brick elevations regarded as solid and permanent well into the twentieth century, now stands beside the Lagan an empty and decaying shell – all that remains of the empire that was Messrs. William Barbour & Sons, Limited. Barbour Threads ceased production and closed on Friday, 27 May 2006. The *Pictorial World* from 1888–89 provides this snapshot of former glory:

> One of the great firms, not alone in Ireland, or even of the United Kingdom, but of the world, is that of William Barbour & Sons, Limited, flax spinners, linen thread and shoe thread manufacturers, yarn dyers and bleachers.
>
> All travellers upon the Great Northern Railway who wish well to Ireland cannot, as they either approach or leave Belfast, but look over with a feeling alike of pride and delight at the Hilden Mills, the headquarters of this renowned firm. That "golden vale of Ulster" is replete alike with rich natural scenery and splendid examples of north of Ireland enterprise; and, standing out prominently amongst the latter are the great mills of the Messrs. Barbour …

The Barbour mill complex extended to over forty-five acres and five hundred workers' cottages covered a further six acres. William Barbour first developed this site in 1823 and a wide range of industrial buildings and machinery was added over the years. William Barbour & Sons Ltd first started the spinning of flax by machinery in 1842. This machinery was driven by an old water wheel but later power engines took over. In 1858 two storeys were added to the old mill and a new mill was started in 1862. The Hilden plant, in 1888, represented manufacturing on a grand scale and provided long term employment over a wide area; the thread factory alone gave employment to over 1,500 women and girls. In addition, the mill boosted the local economy by providing a ready market for Irish flax growers, but large imports of flax from the continent were still required to meet the worldwide demand for the products.

(FGW)

Barbour's Hilden Mills.
(ILC & LM)

The bundled flax was brought into large receiving warehouses where it was stacked and sorted. It was then taken to the hackling room where machines stripped the fibre from the stalk and the process of combing out the strands commenced. This operation was completed in the hand hackling rooms. The flax was then converted into a tape-like form on the spread board and the next process stretched these bands and combined

(JSH)

several into one, which prepared it for the spinning frames. The flax acquired a slight twist during the spinning process and to complete this, and make it into thread, numbers of strands were twisted together. Depending on its future use, four-cord, six-cord or more strands were twisted together, sometimes using very delicate machinery invented by the firm. The thread was then taken to the skeining room where it was wound into specified lengths and tied up ready for dyeing. It was first boiled in large cauldrons to remove all impurities, and then passed into dye vats to be coloured in the dyeing sheds. The red dye required for a particular class of carpet thread involved some fifteen different processes. The thread passed to the drying house and then required to be finished to give it a gloss. The system for finishing thread was originally a tedious labour-intensive process until Samuel Barbour invented a machine called the 'iron man', which was capable of matching the output of eighty operatives.

Barbour's produced linen lace and crochet threads, spool threads for tailors for hand sewing and for use in sewing machines, and they were renowned for the quality of their shoe-threads, which they produced to suit various types of shoe machines. In addition to the Hilden mill the firm had mills at Sprucefield and Dunmurry and employed about 5,000 people in Ireland. The Barbour trademark, the red hand with the word 'Flax' written on the palm, achieved world recognition as the mark of quality. In 2006, the Hilden Mill site ceased production as the owners, the Coats (UK) group, transferred the manufacture of speciality threads for the automotive, upholstery and bedding industries to its sites in Turkey and Hungary.

Counting house and thread factory, Hilden.
(FGW)

The buildings from the Barbour era are impressive, even in decay. Some buildings are deserving of restoration and two in particular attract attention. The red painted thread factory, three-and-a-half storeys high, is built in random stone, with brick detailing, and carries the date 1861 on a keystone above the door. Beside it stands the smooth, stucco finished, counting house, a two-storey block with four tall chimneys above the parapet. An interesting group of gentlemen form the keystones of each building. A remarkable collection of unrecorded subjects who wait patiently, wondering, no doubt, if the listed building status of their home will ensure their survival. Not far away another group of keystone-heads watch and wait and on the sidewall of the engine-house we have an unusual collection for Hilden; the head and trunk of an elephant, a lion's head and a boar's head. Above everything a high tower advertises the Barbour Threads Limited of yesterday with a ghost image painted in red and black capitals, the red hand almost bleached white.

Sir William McIlroy

WILLIAM MCILROY, WHO LIVED in Hilden Cottage, had a very successful career with the Barbour organisation. William, like his father before him, was engaged in the flax trade all his life. The family was originally from the Falls Road, Belfast, but settled for a time in Courtrai, the famous Belgian flax growing district where William's father, James, died on the 8 August 1875 and the family returned home. Educated at St. Malachy's College, Belfast, the young McIlroy served his apprenticeship in the flax department of Barbour's Mill at Hilden. In his spare time he was active with Hilden Athletic Club and played football for Hertford, a popular local team with a large following. William McIlroy was appointed a flax buyer and later promoted to Flax Manager. He was chauffeur-driven in a green Riley car by Joseph Mulholland, resplendent in his green uniform and peaked cap. With the formation of the Linen Thread Co. he was responsible for all flax purchases made by the combine from 1904 until his retirement in 1933. He was an acknowledged authority on flax and there were few superior judges of it in the British Isles. In the course of his duties he travelled to many parts of the world and spoke several languages fluently. He was a JP and a member of the management committee of the County Antrim Infirmary. He died on 5 May 1945 having attended the funeral of his only surviving sister just a few weeks earlier. His two brothers, James and Edward and his other sister, Elizabeth, had all predeceased him.

William McIlroy was a devout Catholic and supported the church and its institutions with numerous benefactions, such as the building of the church of St Mary of the Angels, Clanvaraghan, Drumaroad, Co. Down; St Anthony and St Anne statues, a Lourdes grotto and a Calvary grotto at St. Patrick's, Lisburn; financing new x-ray equipment at the Mater Hospital; annual excursions for Lisburn Boys' School; and the McIlroy burse, value £3,000, at St Malachy's College. In recognition of his good work he was created a Knight of St Gregory the Great by Pope Pius XI. The Order of St. Gregory

A Knight of St. Gregory the Great.

Left: The knight's bi-cornered hat and court sword.

The McIlroy memorial.
(JSH)

is bestowed on persons who distinguish themselves for conspicuous virtue and notable accomplishment on behalf of the church and society, regardless of their religious belief. During his funeral service in St. Patrick's in May 1945 his Knight's bi-cornered hat with plume and court sword were placed on the coffin. He was buried in the family grave at Holy Trinity Cemetery, Longstone Street, Lisburn. Sir Milne Barbour and Mr J.D. Barbour attended his funeral. Two stained glass windows erected by William McIlroy in memory of members of the McIlroy family adorn St. Patrick's Church.

Robert Stewart and Sons

Travellers on the Great Northern Railway, approaching Lisburn railway station in the past, had a fine view of the flax spinning mills and thread manufacturing works of Robert Stewart & Sons. The history of this company as flax spinners and linen and shoe thread manufacturers commenced in the year 1835, when Robert Stewart, Senior, of Lisburn began twisting thread here by hand. In 1845 the firm traded as Robert Stewart & Sons Limited when Mr Stewart took his sons Robert and James Andrew into partnership. Robert Stewart, Senior, died in 1858, but the business was continued actively by the brothers until 1882, when Robert Stewart, Junior, died, leaving James Andrew as the sole proprietor.

Stewart's Mill at night.
(ILC & LM)

Many extensions were carried out during the life-time of Robert Stewart, Junior, and the continued growth of the business required the erection of an entirely new spinning mill, which was completed in 1889.

Robert Stewart's mill.
(ILC & LM)

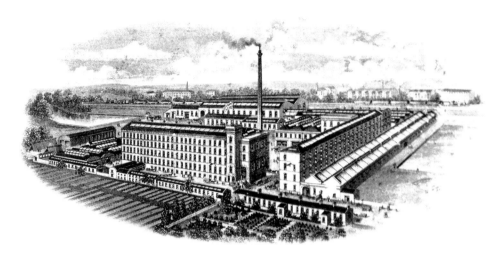

This was 'a handsome structure, built on the most modern designs and fitted throughout with the most approved sanitary arrangements. The comfort of the workers is ensured by the installation of the most efficient ventilating arrangements. The works are lighted throughout by electricity and employ almost 1,000 hands, a large proportion of which are females' (*A Concise History of Lisburn and Neighbourhood*, 1906). McLaughlin & Harvey were contractors to Stewarts from 1874.

The business suffered from the down-turn in the linen industry in 1896, became bankrupt and was eventually purchased by the Linen Thread Co. Ltd.

(ILC & LM)

Special waxed thread was used for the manufacture of golf clubs. *(JSH)*

The Island Spinning Company

Aɴ island site in the middle of the River Lagan, now occupied by Lagan Valley Island, the council entertainment complex, was known as Vitriol Island, the location of a chemical works which manufactured a dilute sulphuric acid, then known as 'oil of vitriol'. This chemical replaced the use of buttermilk in the bleaching of linen in the 1760s and by the close of the century a new bleaching liquor, derived from chlorine, reduced the time required for souring the 'brown linen' from several weeks to a single day.

An aerial view of the Island Spinning Mill.
(ILC & LM)

Samuel Richardson bought the old chemical works and put up a flax spinning mill with a capacity for 2,400 spindles in 1840. He died in 1847 and was succeeded by his brother, J.J. Richardson, who greatly enlarged the mill and added a further 9,500 spindles. Further expansion resulted in an increase in the size of the mill by a quarter in 1885. The production of all kinds of linen thread for hand and machine sewing was an important feature of the company by 1882: it established a high reputation and won many medals and prizes. Before that, in 1871 a weaving factory, for the production of linens, frills, etc., was built to accommodate 240 power looms. The 'Island' extended to a little over three acres and was virtually covered by extensive buildings constructed of stone, brick and iron. Steam power had arrived and drove three compound engines and a single cylinder beam engine. A large part of the works was lit by electricity. Coal was supplied by horse-drawn lighters from the quays in Belfast along the canal.

By 1888 the Island Spinning Co.'s employees numbered about 1,100 and many of them lived in houses supplied by the company. These workers' houses had a water supply laid on

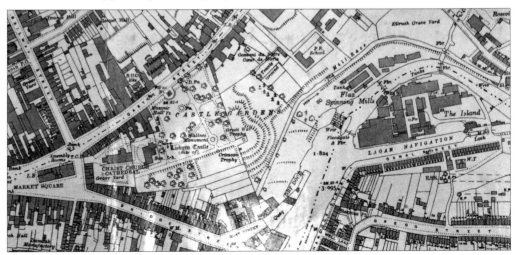

The Island Spinning Company mills on the Lagan Navigation Canal.
(BCL)

from an artesian well on the island, which was pumped to a fountain on the roadway. Conditions for labour were continually improving; a comfortable dining hall was supplied for the workers in 1884, under the guidance of the chairman, Mr. Joseph Richardson and the managing director, George H. Clarke.

(ILC & LM)

Production at the mill came to an end in 1983 and Lisburn Borough Council purchased the site. Today, all along the Lagan valley the impressive brick structures of a past industrial age are in decay, and are about to be or have already been demolished: in this case the warmth of traditional brickwork, which seemed to blend with the natural landscape, has been replaced by Portland stone, a questionable upgrade and forever an import.

A postcard showing the Island Spinning Company.
(JSH)

Richardson Sons & Owden Limited

James Nicholson
Richardson
(1782–1847).

The Richardson name is synonymous with the linen industry in Ulster. John Richardson (1719–1759) was descended from a Warwickshire family that settled in Loughgall in the seventeenth century. He served his time to the linen trade with his relatives, the Hoggs of Lisburn, and settled there permanently when he married Ruth, the daughter of William Hogg, who had a bleach green at Glenmore. The family lived in Castle Street, where their son Jonathan was born in 1756. Jonathan Richardson (1756–1817) was among the most enterprising linen merchants of his day. He carried out trials and experiments which enabled him to run his bleach works all the year round. Jonathan married Sarah Nicholson, and their son James Nicholson Richardson (1782–1847) was the founder of Richardson Sons & Owden Ltd. He purchased Lambeg House in 1835 and changed the name to Glenmore, the name associated with the area. His house was partly screened from his business interest by a belt of trees.

The firm had three large bleachworks known as Upper Glenmore, Lower Glenmore and Millbrook, where the beetling and finishing works were situated. In addition to the works at Lisburn the firm had weaving factories in Co. Down and spinning mills and weaving factories in Co. Armagh. Their headquarters building was in Belfast. Their works and premises were equipped with all the facilities of a major enterprise and by the 1890s their factories and offices provided employment for about 7,000 workers.

James Nicholson Richardson married Anna Grubb, from Anner Mills, near Clonmel, Co. Tipperary. The couple were consistent and devoted members of the Society of Friends and closely observed the Quaker customs and dress of the day. A family story tells of a visit to the north of Ireland by Ibrahim Pasha, Khedive of Egypt, to look into the growth of flax and the linen industry. Among other places, he visited the bleach works at Glenmore, arriving there on a Sunday, but James N. Richardson politely declined to gather the men and start the machinery on the day of rest. The Khedive respected his scruples and was quite civil about it.

Under his guidance and direction, the Richardson family linen business grew and prospered and in 1825 he took into partnership John Owden, and founded the firm of J.N. Richardson Sons & Owden Ltd., although his sons were not of age at that date. John Owden came as a young man from England, his family was of Huguenot descent; his brother Sir Thomas Owden had been Lord Mayor of London. James N. Richardson gradually left the management of the business to John Owden and his sons as they reached maturity.

James Nicholson Richardson lived until 1847 but he had relinquished active direction of the business some time before that date. He left seven sons, many of them men of distinction in the linen trade. Jonathan Richardson (1811–1869), the eldest son, retained his financial interest in the family business but preferred the life of a country gentleman and politician. Unlike his father, the strict rules of the Society of Friends did not appeal to him and he became an enthusiastic member of the Church of Ireland. His son, Charles Herbert

Richardson, D.L., J.P., of Cedarhurst, Belfast, was for some years chairman and managing director of Richardson Sons & Owden Ltd., until his death in 1931.

Nothing remains of the Glenmore complex, but most of us are familiar with the magnificent warehouse, erected in 1869, that was the former headquarters of Messrs. Richardson Sons & Owden Ltd.; we know it as the Marks and Spencer building, previously the Water Office in Donegall Square, Belfast. *Industries of Ireland* 1891 had this to say about Richardson's products:

Richardson Sons, & Owden Ltd. warehouse, Donegall Square North, Belfast, designed by W.H. Lynn and built in 1867–1869.
(PRONI D/2826/64/7)

The stocks are simply indescribable in their varied characteristics of beauty and intrinsic worth, and are typical of the firm, whose fame has been won and maintained by the unvarying perfection of its products. For more than a hundred years Messrs. Richardson Sons & Owden have manufactured linen fabrics noted for superiority of texture, finish, quality, and design, and in such lines as plain linens, sheetings, pillow linens, towels, diapers, handkerchiefs, fine damask cloths, and artistic embroidered goods of every kind. They enjoy a reputation which has been equalled by very few of their contemporaries, and excelled by none. Irish linens are foremost among the flax-woven textiles of the world, and Messrs. Richardson Sons & Owden Limited stand admittedly among the most advanced leaders of the Irish linen trade. Their trade-mark (a lion rampant – the crest of the Richardson family) is known and respected the wide world over, and 'Richardson's linens', as a domestic and commercial term, is a household word at home and abroad, and a synonym for the highest excellence in linen cloths.

The warehouse building was gutted internally in the Blitz and after the war the original steep roof and elaborate dormers were replaced by a flat roof. The Marks & Spencer 1985 restoration included a limited mock reconstruction of the roof. *(RWP)*

In 1920, Glenmore House, the former home of James Nicholson Richardson, became home to the Linen Research Institute, when the government-backed Linen Industry Research Association was formed. The house and a range of outbuildings and workshops were used as offices and technical laboratories where research into the linen manufacturing process, from flax culture to the final stages of bleaching, dyeing and finishing of the fabric, was carried out. The declining linen industry could not support a research association, which was forced to close, and the property was sold in 1993.

History in Stained Glass

Memorial window to William Barbour (1797–1875), the founder of Hilden Mill, and his wife Eliza Kennedy. First Lisburn Presbyterian Church. *(FGW)*

The Barbour commemorative window, Lisburn Cathedral, designed by William Morris and Co. London. Sir John Milne Barbour dedicated the window to his wife Eliza and their son, John Milne Jr., who died in an aviation accident. Sir Milne was the chairman of the Linen Thread Co., MP for South Antrim and a Minister in the Northern Ireland Parliament. The central feature is Christ the King, surrounded by Saints and Martyrs from church history. *(JSH)*

Stained glass window, Church of St. Colman, Queensway, Lambeg, designed by Neil Shawcross for the Hilden studios of CWS Design. *(FGW)*

Gallery window detail, Christ Church Derriaghy. Dedicated by Maria Corken in memory of her husband Rev. John Corken (1798–1834) and their three sons. Maria was the daughter of the Rev Snowden Cupples, Rector of Lisburn Cathedral. *(FGW)*

Memorial window in memory of Captain Cecil F. K. Ewart, company commander with the 1st Lisburn Battalion, Ulster Volunteer Force, killed-in-action serving with 11 Royal Irish Rifles near Thiepval Wood on the Somme 1 July 1916. Christ Church, Lisburn. *(FGW)*

The William McIlroy windows. St.Patrick's, Lisburn. *(JSH)*

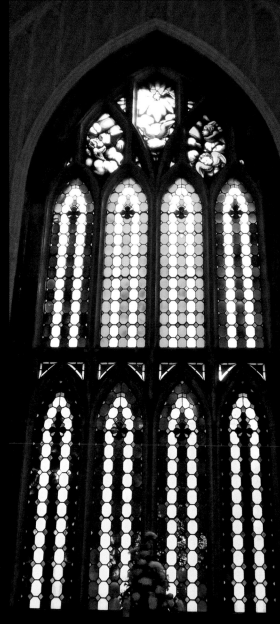

Hillsborough Parish Church, east window. The upper portion is said to have been designed by Sir Joshua Reynolds. The colours are those of the church calendar. *(JSH)*

The Resurrection window, First Lisburn Presbyterian Church commemorates the restoration of the church and halls following a bomb-blast on 5 August 1981. It is crafted from fragments of the old windows. *(JSH)*

Memorial window, Eglantine Parish Church, installed and dedicated in 1990, to mark the 50th Anniversary of the Battle of Britain. *(JSH)*

Below: Memorial window to John Doherty Barbour (1824–1901) of Hilden and Conway. His vision led to the formation of the Linen Thread Co. Ltd. in 1898. Hillhall Presbyterian Church. *(FGW)*

Rev. Saumarez Dubourdieu

Rev. Saumarez
Dubourdieu.
(JSH)

THE REV. SAUMAREZ DUBOURDIEU (1717–1812), minister of the French Protestant Church in Lisburn and for fifty-six years master of the classical school in Bow Street, is commemorated on a monument in Lisburn Cathedral erected by his former scholars. The monument, executed by John Smyth of Dublin, is in white marble, a bust standing on a handsome sarcophagus. Some years ago, the bust became separated from the wall tablet and the sarcophagus but, thanks to Lottery funding, the monument was professionally cleaned, restored and re-mounted in its original position. Part of the monument inscription reads in translation, 'descended from French parentage, who had been forced into exile, by religious persecution, he earned for himself on merit, a name, a habitation and a new country among strangers.'

The religious persecution in France during the seventeenth century provides the backdrop. The Huguenots were French Protestants who followed the teachings of John Calvin (1509–64) and formed the Reformed Church of France. Their new reformed faith brought them into theological conflict with the Catholic Church and the State: persecution and open hostility led to the French Wars of Religion, which lasted for thirty-five years. In 1598, the wars ended when Henry of Navarre changed his religion so that he could become King of France, and with the signing of the Edict of Nantes he provided a degree of religious freedom for the Huguenots, his former co-religionists. The Revocation of the Edict of Nantes by Louis XIV in October 1685 proscribed the Protestant religion and introduced the most severe penalties. The choice for the Huguenots was stark, either abandon the practice of their religion, become Roman Catholics or go into exile. The Dubourdieu family chose exile.

Saumarez Dubourdieu was the son of the Rev. Jean Armand Dubourdieu (1683–1723) and the Countess D'Espouage. His grandmother, the widow of James Dubourdieu (1640?–1683), fled from the persecution in France by disguising herself as a peasant, to escape the frontier guards, and crossing into German-Switzerland with her infant son, Jean Armand, hidden in a shawl on her back. They made their way to London. Jean Armand Dubourdieu became minister of the Savoy church in London and chaplain to the Duke of Richmond and Lennox. He was the author of an acclaimed book of sermons in French and held a respected position in the church.

Marble relief memorial
to Rev. Saumarez
Dubourdieu. *(JSH)*

His son, Saumarez Dubourdieu, went to Dublin and was brought up by his grandmother. He was a classical scholar at Trinity College and in 1756 he came to Lisburn and opened a classical school in Bow Street, which was highly regarded. The Rev. Charles De La Valade, who was chaplain to the French colony there, and a brother of Saumarez's grandmother, may have influenced his move to Lisburn. When his great-uncle died, he succeeded him as minister of the French church in Lisburn, which stood on the site of the old Town Hall in Castle Street. His gravestone, a badly cracked flat slab laid in Lambeg churchyard bears this inscription.

HERE LIETH THE BODY OF THE REVEREND
SAUMAREZ DUBOURDIEU, A.M.
WHO WAS FIFTY YEARS OFFICIATING CLERGYMAN
OF THIS PARISH
AND FOR A LONGER PERIOD, MINISTER OF THE
FRENCH PROTESTANT CHURCH OF LISBURN.
SUBSEQUENTLY VICAR OF THE PARISH OF GLENAVY.
HE WAS ALSO MASTER OF THE CLASSICAL SCHOOL OF
LISBURN.
THE YOUTH COMMITTED TO HIS CARE
HE INSTRUCTED IN USEFUL AND IN ORNAMENTAL
LEARNING,
THE FLOCK OF WHICH HE WAS THE PASTOR
IN THE TRUE PRINCIPLES OF THE CHRISTAIN FAITH,
AND ALL WHO WITNESSED HIS CONDUCT
BY THE BRIGHT EXAMPLE OF A WELL-SPENT
LIFE.
HE DIED ON THE 14th DAY OF DECEMBER 1812,
AGED 96 YEARS AND 3 MONTHS.
HIS GRATEFUL SCHOLARS
IN REMEMBRANCE OF HIS VIRTUE
HAVE CAUSED THIS STONE TO BE DEDICATED TO HIS
MEMORY
ALSO, A MONUMENT MORE SUITABLE TO HIS
MERITS AND TO THEIR GRATITUDE
IN THE PARISH CHURCH
OF
LISBURN.

Saumarez Dubourdieu and his family lived and put down roots in the area around Lisburn, but he was not the first member of this noted family to have travelled this way. Jean Dubourdieu, his great-uncle who had helped his grandmother escape from France, was the first to arrive here, while serving with the Williamite army in Ireland. He was chaplain to the Duke of Schomberg and ministered to the Huguenot regiments during the winter of 1689–90, when Schomberg made Lisburn his headquarters. He saw action at the Battle of the Boyne and it is claimed that he cradled Schomberg in his arms when he was shot and fell mortally wounded from his horse. Dubourdieu continued in service with Charles, the second Duke of Schomberg, but when the Duke died in Turin in 1693 he moved to London. He was a respected preacher and writer and on his death in 1722 he was interred in the Church of the Savoy in London.

The main burial ground for members of the French church in Lisburn was Christ Church Cathedral graveyard. We give verses from a poem entitled *On the Graves of French Protestants in Lisburn Churchyard,* found in an old scrap book formed about the time of Waterloo – it is preceded by this note:

> In the south-east corner of Lisburn churchyard are a few weather worn tombstones, the sole memorial of a colony of Huguenot exiles.

On the Graves of French Protestants in Lisburn Churchyard

Lightly tread! Beneath are sleeping,
Warriors of the Cross of God.
Warriors, conscience boldly keeping,
Spite of persecutor's rod;
Warriors on their God relying;
Warriors – victors over Rome;
Kings whom glories never dying,
Wait in an eternal home.

Faithful like their sires before them,
To the faith their souls had tried,
Vainly bigot power o'erbore them,
Courtly arts in vain were plied.
Danger scorning, bribes despising
Wealth and lands they left behind,
More than gold their conscience prizing,
More than home their chainless mind.

Northmen, Northmen – mark the preaching,
Of the men who would not lie;
Hear the faithful exiles teaching,
Wisdom that can never die.
Trust not man, for man betrayed you,
Trust not Rome for friendship slays.
Trust in God; with him to aid you
Ye shall stand when Rome decays.

Lisburn Golf Club

(JSH)

WHILE IT IS GENERALLY recognised that Lisburn Golf Club was founded in 1905 and celebrated its centenary in 2005, not everyone is aware that a golf club existed in Lisburn at an earlier date. This first club was formed in 1890 and the game of golf was played over a course almost identical in layout to the later course. It is interesting to follow the history of the intervening years.

A meeting, held to discuss the founding of the Manor House Golf Club, Lisburn, was held in 1890, probably in the month of November. The name, Manor House, was chosen to indicate to potential members that this was to be a town club, rather than a club formed by a few local worthies wishing to take part in a new sport. This name transferred over from the Manor House lands and a lease on the property was secured from Miss Stannus, daughter of Walter Trevor Stannus, agent of the Marquess of Hertford. The gate lodge of the former main entrance survives at Manor Drive, Lisburn.

The members engaged the well-known golf course designer Mr. G.L. Baillie, who had by this time laid out courses at Royal Belfast Golf Club (1881), the County Golf Club, Portrush (1888) and the County Down Club at Newcastle (1889). Mr Baillie is often credited with being responsible for bringing the game of golf to Ulster. Baillie laid out a nine-hole course and it was open for play on the 18 March 1891, when the club became known as Lisburn Golf Club. It was open to ladies from its inception. The annual subscription was one guinea – ladies half price. This date marks the club's official founding and in 1894 it became affiliated to the Golfing Union of Ireland, (GUI), the oldest golfing union in the world. Later that year the GUI decided that the twenty-one-member clubs should be divided into groups to promote inter-club matches. This heralded the birth of All-Ireland Cups and Shields, such as the Senior and Junior Cups. Lisburn was in a group comprising Belmont (Belfast), Dungannon and County Down.

The Ladies' section of the club was much more active and more enthusiastic than the men's. This was probably due to the fact, that at that time it was more difficult for men to take time off work, and, because the available grass cutting machinery could not cope with the summer growth, the course was only open for play during the winter months. At the inaugural meeting of the Irish Ladies' Golfing Union in December 1893, three ladies from Lisburn Golf Club attended the meeting, which was held at the Girls' Friendly Society Lodge, Belfast. One of the Lisburn ladies, Miss Nellie Graham, was elected one of the Vice-presidents. She must have been a good golfer as she won the Irish Ladies' Championship in 1896, when she defeated Miss E. Brownrigg

MISS N. GRAHAM.
Irish Champion, 1896-7.

The Irish Golfer, 1899

at Newcastle by 4 and 3, and the following year at Dollymount, Dublin, she defeated Miss Magill by the same margin. Her best victory was reserved for the British Ladies' Championship at Aberdovey in 1901, when she defeated the renowned Rhona Adair in the final, 3 and 1.

Postcard from the 1930s showing the clubhouse and the ninth green. *(JSH)*

Fred Daly, the 1947 Open Champion, when qualifying for the 1952 News of the World Match-play Championship, set a new course record for professionals with a round of 66. He was later to win the title. The record score for the nine-hole course was set by an amateur, Mr. Harry Connolly, in May 1934.

With only winter play permitted and no golf on Sundays the club was facing difficulties from the beginning. It ceased to exist for a number of years. In April 1905, a meeting was held in Lisburn Courthouse to consider reforming a golf club and later that year the course was in play, with Lisburn Golf Club again affiliated to the Golfing Union of Ireland. This explains why the Club centenary was only celebrated in 2005.

In 1973 the club decided to move; the Chapel Hill course was surrounded by housing and difficulties were experienced in maintaining the course boundaries. The decision was taken to sell the course to the Borough Council for £110,000 and purchase 120 acres of land at Blaris Lodge for £67,000. Blaris Lodge was originally built in the early part of the 20th century by the Marquis of Downshire as a residence for his doctor to ensure that he was within easy reach of Hillsborough Castle. It was eventually demolished in 1987. A few shots were played on the Blaris course before it opened. The Governor of Northern Ireland, Lord Grey, attended on the 6 July 1972 and played a ball up the first fairway. Lord Grey promised to return to perform the opening ceremony at a later date, a commitment he was unable to fulfil due to his untimely departure from Northern Ireland.

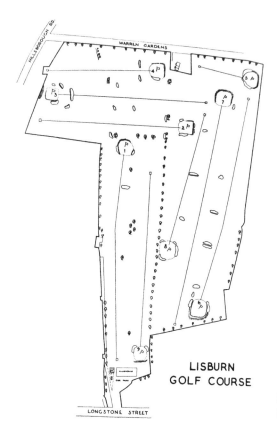

LISBURN GOLF COURSE

Manor House Golf Club with entrance from Longstone Street. *(JSH)*

Sir Richard Wallace

RICHARD WALLACE WAS BORN Richard Jackson, the illegitimate son of the 4th Marquess of Hertford and Mrs Agnes Jackson. Born in London on 21 June 1818, he was raised in Paris by his grandmother from the age of six. The 4th Marquess never acknowledged his paternity, and in 1842 Richard took his mother's maiden name, rejecting the name 'Jackson' and taking that of Wallace. Until his father's death he acted as the 4th Marquess's sale-room assistant and adviser. In 1870 he inherited his father's art collection, the Rue Laffitte apartment in Paris, Bagatelle, a chateau in the Bois de Boulogne and estates in Ireland. He also bought the lease of Hertford House, London, from the 5th Marquess.

Sir Richard Wallace Bart, K.G.B. Wallace is wearing evening dress with the Cross of the Order of the Bath around his neck and the Star on his breast. From an original bust by E. Hannaux
(ILC & LM)

When Paris was besieged by the Prussians and then devastated by the uprising of the Commune, Wallace gained a considerable reputation for his charitable works and gifts to humanitarian causes. He used his large reserves of capital to protect the English-speaking community in Paris and distributed money to impoverished districts of the city to relieve suffering. He set an example of courage and bravery in the face of adversity which bolstered the morale of the people. In recognition of his philanthropy Queen Victoria conferred on him a baronetcy in 1871, just after he had married his mistress, Julie Castelnau, the mother of his thirty-year-old son, Edmond Richard.

In 1872, he took up residence in London, bringing with him from Paris many of his finest works of art. Much of the collection was exhibited at the Bethnal Green Museum where it was a popular sensation, visited by millions of people. The exhibition was opened by the Prince of Wales, which was the start of a close friendship between the two men. The success of this event added to the stature and reputation of Richard Wallace. Unlike his father, he took an interest in the responsibilities that his wealth brought him, particularly in the Lisburn estate. He received a rapturous welcome on his first visit to Lisburn on 14 February 1873, but the circumstances of his birth and the refusal of his wife and son to become anglicized meant that he was never fully accepted in English society. After the death of his son in 1887 he spent an increasing amount of time alone at Bagatelle. He died here on 20 July 1890 and was buried in the Hertford family vault in the cemetery of Pere Lachaise.

Wallace Heritage in Lisburn

S IR RICHARD WALLACE BECAME the Member of Parliament for Lisburn in 1873 and
served as MP until 1884, when Lisburn's right to its own MP was removed and the town
was merged in a new constituency called South Antrim. He declined the nomination for the

Castle House
(ILC & LM)

new electoral division. Sir Richard took a great interest in the town
and was its principal benefactor, improving both the amenities
and appearance and encouraging development. The old market
house was remodelled and upgraded as the Assembly Rooms.
The Union Bridge leading to the County Down, was improved
and strengthened; the town's water supply up-graded and its
reservoir enlarged. He provided a site for the Temperance Institute
in Railway Street and converted a meadow into a twenty-six acre
People's Park, now Wallace Park, at a cost of £4,000. In 1880, he
funded the Lisburn University and Intermediate School, on a site
fronting the Antrim Road, now named Wallace High School in his memory. The school
takes the Hertford motto 'Esperance'. Sir Richard built a magnificent Italianate courthouse
beside the railway station at a cost of £4,000. It opened in 1884 and was demolished in
1971, an act of corporate vandalism. Its inauspicious successor has long passed its sell
by date. Wallace employed the architect Thomas Ambler, who had remodelled Hertford
House for him, to build a house in Lisburn, called Castle House. The result, an imposing
two-storey red brick mansion with stone dressings and a mansard roof cost over £20,000.
Wallace had hoped that his son Edmond would take up residence in Lisburn, but this was
not to be, and Castle House was only rarely used. In 1914 it was acquired by the town
and used as the Technical College. Today, its successor, the Lisburn campus of the South
Eastern Regional College, (SERC), presents an uninspiring elevation to Castle Street. Is
Castle House in need of protection?

Following his death in 1890 the citizens of Lisburn erected, by subscription, a memorial
to Sir Richard in Castle Gardens. The monument, which was designed by the Belfast
company, Robinson and Co., carries this inscription: 'to perpetuate the memory of one
whose delight was to do good and in grateful recognition of his generous interest in the
prosperity of this town'. Castle Gardens was given to the town council by Lady Wallace's
heir, Sir John Murray Scott in 1901. Recently the gardens have been restored with the
assistance of the Heritage Lottery Fund. Castle Gardens comprises a 19th century town
park that incorporates older 17th century terraces. The steeply sloping terraces run down
to the river Lagan, while the Victorian park on the upper level forms the frontage to Castle
House. Archaeological investigations, which provided an insight into early garden design,
exposed the Perron – a grand double staircase leading from the centre of the bowling
green onto the terrace; the Turret – a semi-circular look-out tower located on the topmost
terrace and the Gazebo surviving below the bowling green. Listed structures in the park

that have been restored include the Egret Fountain of circa 1870, a cannon of Crimean War vintage, which carries the inscription: 'This gun taken at Sebastopol was presented to the town of Lisburn by Admiral Meynell. R.N. 1858', and the Wallace Fountain. The Wallace Fountain we can inspect at close quarters.

The Wallace Fountain

ORIGINALLY KNOWN AS 'LES Wallaces', drinking fountains were a generous gift to the people of Paris by Richard Wallace, who was living in Paris at the time of the Franco-Prussian War, 1870–1871. There was a long siege of Paris and when it ended Wallace was made aware of the lack of free water due to damage to aqueducts in the city. He decided to commission fountains to be sited all over the city. In the end there were over fifty fountains in use. He wanted the fountains to be both practical and attractive.

Sir Richard presented five fountains to Lisburn in 1876. They were originally located at the junction of Market Place with Bow Street; in Market Square; in Castle Gardens; in Wallace Park and at the junction of Seymour Street, Low Road and Millbrook in front of Seymour Street Methodist Church. Only two survive to this day; three of the fountains were scrapped to assist the war effort. How many times have you walked past a green fountain? Pause for a moment and observe art and mythology entwined.

(JSH)

The base of the fountain is a Greek cross plinth from which the pedestal rises. An elaborate console, decorated with a scallop shell from which pearls flow, separates four panels on which a water serpent is coiled around a trident. The trident is associated with the mythological Poseidon, the protector of all waters. A scallop is symbolic of baptism and fertility, and pearls represent purity and wisdom. A cornice displays the name of the manufacturer, Val D'Osne, and records the name of the sculptor, Ch. Lebourg SC/1872 – Charles Lebourg.

Four nymphs or caryatids with raised arms support a fish-scale dome with a fleur-de-lys cornice. Four dolphins with entwined tails at the apex are a symbolic protector of all things related to water. The statues represent kindness, simplicity, charity and sobriety (at a time when the Temperance Movement was active). They also represent the four seasons: Simplicity symbolizes spring, Charity: summer, Sobriety: autumn and Kindness: winter. Look closely – the statues differ slightly from each other: some have their eyes closed; whereas with others the eyes are open. There are differences in the position of the knee and feet and in the manner of the dress. Originally, in a working fountain, a stream of water from a tap in the dome cascaded into the basin below. Tin cups were provided for drinking, securely chained to the fountain, before public hygiene became a concern.

Good Samaritan window. *(JSH)*

Castle Gardens provides a vantage point from which to appreciate the strategic siting of the old castle above the Lagan and an opportunity to contrast the aesthetic quality and balance of the design of Castle House behind us, with the modern architecture of the Civic Centre below, which displays many quality short comings. The planning authorities should insist on a Wallace legacy of good taste. In Lisburn we have new housing developments – Sir Richard or Lady Wallace Park, Drive, Square, Lane and the like – they owe much to the business acumen of the housing marketing executive in perpetuating the Wallace name, if not the architectural refinement of a bygone age.

Lisburn Cathedral adjoins the gardens and Sir Richard contributed to extensive renovation work there. On the southern wall of the chancel and the nave are two stained-glass windows, dedicated to him, which display the excellence attained by Mayer & Co. of Munich and London. One illustrates Sir Richard's charitable work to the afflicted – 'giving bread to the hungry and drink to the thirsty.' This window was erected by the congregation of the Cathedral and other friends, including H.R.H. Albert Edward, Prince of Wales. The other window depicts the parable of the Good Samaritan entreating us 'to go and do thou likewise'. This was erected by his widow, Lady Wallace.

On her death in 1897 she bequeathed Sir Richard's extensive art collection to the nation. Known as The Wallace Collection, it is housed in Hertford House, London. Interestingly, by the terms of Lady Wallace's will, it is a 'closed' collection in that nothing may be added or taken away.

Wallace Park

WALLACE PARK IS THE premier park in Lisburn and is often the centre for civic, social and sporting events. Originally called the People's Park, the twenty-six acres of land was a gift from Sir Richard Wallace to the people of Lisburn. Following his death in 1890 the name was changed to 'Wallace Park' in his memory. The Grant, dated 22 June 1885, stated that Sir Richard Wallace had 'freely and voluntarily agreed to grant and convey the piece or parcel of land… as and for a public park or recreation ground for the inhabitants of the Borough or Town of Lisburn.' Sir Richard's benefaction was for the enjoyment of the good citizens of Lisburn; the local Councillors were the trustees. It still is the People's Park

– a twenty-first century council suggestion that a private club should build its own facilities in the park, triggered a negative public reaction supported by a petition containing over 3,000 signatures, which demonstrated the strength of feeling that this is 'Public' space.

The park is officially designated an Historic Park and Garden and contains features of architectural and historic interest. It was formed at a cost of £4,000 and Sir Richard financed the building of the bandstand, entrance gates and gate lodges. The cricket ground, also the gift of Sir Richard Wallace, dates from 1854, although cricket in Lisburn dates back to 1836. Boundary stones inscribed 'R W' are at the four corners of the cricket pitch. Lisburn Cricket Club is the oldest cricket club in Northern Ireland having been established in 1836. It is the third oldest in Ireland after Phoenix C.C. (1830) and Dublin University (1835). The pond on the elevated site at Fort Hill is the original old town reservoir, which supplied water to the town through wooden pipes. The landscaped and grassed remains of a velodrome are all that survives of a bygone age.

(JSH)

In the late 1890s cycling became very popular with many of the townspeople and a cycle track was laid out in the park. The *Lisburn Herald* carried a report in May 1893 that cyclists were becoming more numerous day by day and Wallace Park was infested with the 'scorchers'. The favourite ride was along the centre walk, the new track being almost completely ignored. The paper offered this explanation:

> Of course this can be partly understood, as a cinder track is considered by the "collar and cuff" gentry too far removed from the favourite promenade of the fair sex, who are thus deprived of admiring the "graceful" pose, staying and driving power of these modern Romeos.

As the popularity of cycling increased the Lisburn Wheeler's Club was formed in 1897. Cycle races took place on this track and later banking was introduced, creating Lisburn's first velodrome.

During the Great War, a portion of the park was allocated as garden plots for food production and the secretary of the cricket club announced that there would be no cricket in 1916 – the club would be letting out the cricket field for the grazing of sheep at a moderate rent! One of the paths, which follows the railway, is called the

Lisburn Bikers, 1909. *(ILC & LM)*

Dean's Walk, a public right of way for over 150 years and the entitlement of the people of Lisburn to pass to and fro is an established part of the history of the town.

The City Council's recent refurbishment of the park has increased its popularity.

Laura Bell – The Island Queen

Lord O'Neill's Cottage,
Ram's Island, Lough
Neagh.
(Dublin Penny Journal, 1833)

IN 1853, HENRY BELL of Grove Cottage, near Lambeg, published a privately printed pamphlet entitled *A Short Visit to Ram's Island, Lough Neagh, and its vicinity in the year 1853*. This publication contained a poem entitled *The Island Queen*, described as Mrs. A.F. Thistlethwayte's farewell to Ram's Island, on her departure for London, having spent some weeks in Lord O'Neill's cottage on the island. 'The Island Queen', Mr. Bell informs us, 'was an honorary title bestowed on Mrs. Thistlethwayte by the residents of the neighbourhood, on the occasion of her welcome visit to this interesting locality, the home of her fathers.' Who was Mrs. A.F. Thistlethwayte?

Mrs. Thistlethwayte (1831?–1894) was the former Miss Laura Bell from Glenavy who left home at an early age, after an unsupervised childhood, and supplemented her income as a shop assistant in Belfast by selective prostitution. Laura moved to Dublin where her finances were secured to the extent that she was able to drive in her own carriage in the Phoenix Park. While in Dublin she was reputed to have had an association with Dr. William Wilde, the father of Oscar Wilde. About 1849, Laura Bell moved to London where her conquest of Jung Bahadur, a Nepalese Prince, established her reputation as a courtesan. Sir Jung Bahadur (1816–1877), prime minister and virtual ruler of Nepal from 1846 to 1877, established the powerful Rana dynasty of heredity prime ministers, an office that remained in his family until 1951. During 1850–51 he visited England and remained a firm friend of the British throughout his life. He kept the country and its Gurkha regiments loyal to the British during the Indian Mutiny of 1857–58. He was admitted to The Order of The Bath for his services. It has been claimed that in the brief time that Laura Bell was his mistress she deprived him of a quarter of a million pounds.

Sir Jung Bahadur, Prime
Minister of Nepal, 1846
–1877.

Sir Francis Burnand, an eminent Victorian, recalls for us the modus operandi of the demi-monde in the London of that time. Laura Bell won widespread admiration for her riding ability which she displayed to advantage in Rotten Row. As Burnand puts it in his personal *Records and Reminiscences*:

As a 'boy about town' I remember several notorious Hetairai being pointed out to me as they rode in spanking style in the Row, were driven in open landaus, or charioteered themselves about Hyde Park in the season. The most memorable of these was Laura Bell ... Clearly do I call to mind Laura Bell's pretty, doll-like face, her big eyes, not ignorant of an artistic touch that added a lustre to their natural brilliancy, and her quick vivacious glances as she sat in an open phaeton, vivaciously talking with a variety of men, all 'swells' of the period of course, at the corner of the drive near the Achilles statue, with her smart little 'tiger' stood at the horses' heads. What strange stories I used to hear of her recklessness, her prodigality, her luxury, and her cleverness.

In 1853, Laura Bell married a man of property, Captain August Frederick Thistlethwayte, with an address at Grosvenor Square, London, and an estate in Ross-shire in Scotland. In the 1860s, Laura Thistlethwayte experienced a religious conversion and became an established woman evangelist, preaching in public and holding evangelical tea parties at her home, which became famous in high society circles. Lady St. Helier, who spent part of the year with an uncle and aunt in Ross-shire near the Thistlethwayte's estate, paints a pen portrait of Laura:

> She was a very striking looking woman, and the large black mantilla which covered her masses of golden hair, the magnificent jewels she wore round her neck, and the flashing rings on her hands with which she gesticulated, added to the soft tones of a very beautiful voice and made a great impression on those who listened to her.

She also provides this colourful description of Laura as a preacher:

> The internal surroundings of the church did not lend themselves to any emotional effect, but Mrs. Thistlethwayte beautifully dressed, and standing at the end of the building so that all the light which entered through the small windows was thrown on her, illuminating the spot where she stood, poured out an impassioned address, eloquent and effective. She spoke with great facility, and with a good deal of emotion in her voice, and with an evident air of sincerity and personal conviction. This added to the remains of very great beauty, an influence largely increased by her great generosity to the poor people, made a vast impression on her congregation, and after the first meetings she succeeded in producing all the effects of other revival preachers, and many conversions were supposed to have been the result of her ministrations.

Encouraged by her success amongst the folk of Ross-shire she moved to a larger centre of population in the town of Dingwall where she ran up against stern opposition of the Free Church minister and the elders of the kirk, who did their best to disrupt the meetings so that they were disjointed and rowdy affairs. She received some support in the columns of the *Inverness Courier* and replies from the Free Church minister were published. To give support was to come under attack. The Free Synod of Moray reported that one of their elders, the Earl of Kintore, 'had been accompanying Mrs Thistlethwayte – thus lending himself to a practice that had been productive of incalculable evil. This female preaching was becoming a perfect scandal – a perfect nuisance – and of late they had too much of it'. Public teaching by a woman in Ross-shire was seen by the Rev. John Kennedy as a startling novelty and plainly anti-scriptural.

Laura Bell as 'The Nun'
by Alfred Clayton.
(By kind permission of Lord Bathurst and the Courtauld Institute of Fine Art. Photographic survey at Courtauld Institute of Art, London)

One letter came from Laura herself:

Dear Sir,
You will favour the cause of truth by kindly stating in your next report that I have not appeared in any pulpit here. At the request of many I have, through grace, humbly declared the plan of salvation by faith in a risen Saviour, the Lord Jesus Christ – my object being to enlighten the poor and not the rich. Dr. Beggs and Mr. Kennedy are both ignorant as to what the true Church of Christ is founded upon. It certainly is not bricks and mortar but living stones bought with the precious blood of a Lamb without a blemish.

She signed her letter with this testimony.

A sinner saved by grace through faith in the Lamb of God – L. Thistlethwayte.

Things were rather different in London as the *Courier*'s London correspondent reported:

Mrs. Thistlethwayte is all the rage as a preacher in town. I went to hear her on Sunday last, but the place was so crowded with fashionables, that admittance was impossible. Sir Edwin Landseer attends her, and I fancy she will have to start a tabernacle of her own and rival Spurgeon.

The author of *Fifty Years of London Society* also makes a comparison with Charles Haddon Spurgeon of the Reformed Baptist tradition.

Her intellectual capacity was almost phenomenal and to this was added a very poetical imagination. Her appearance on the platform of the Polytechnic was a realisation of beauty and art. Mrs. Thistlethwayte was not much inferior to Spurgeon.

Mrs. Thistlethwayte made her home in Grosvenor Square the headquarters of her mission and gave evangelical tea parties, which were famous in London society circles. About this time, she met William Ewart Gladstone, Prime Minister of Britain, who with his wife maintained a friendship with Laura up until her death. Gladstone's association with, and his 'rescue work' with prostitutes is a subject on its own – his political enemies interpreted it in its worst light; his admirers accepted what he himself said – it was an effort to win them away from immoral ways to a nobler and Christian life. The Gladstone Library and Museum at Hawardwen, Wales, holds a large collection of letters written to Laura by Mr Gladstone. His relationship with Mrs Thistlethwayte was important to him because it was to her that he revealed the extent that politics consumed him. Following the death of her husband in 1887, Laura moved to a house in Hampstead where the Gladstones visited her and sometimes stayed. Laura died in 1894 and was buried in the Thistlethwayte's family vault in Paddington Green Cemetery, London.

Was Henry Bell of Lambeg related to Laura Bell? We cannot establish a family connection, but such a link would have provided the incentive for the published tribute to the transformed and now socially acceptable Mrs Thistlethwayte:

> …this amazing woman who first shocked London with her lovely shoulders and her cascading golden hair and went on to rouse the capital to religious fervour with her evangelism and her eloquence.

Laura Bell, miniature on ivory, signed Ernest Girard.
(Trustees of The Wallace Collection)

Lisburn Railway Station

(JSH)

Lisburn Railway Station is unique in the railway history of Northern Ireland as it was the destination for the first train from Belfast. The station was opened on Monday, 12 August 1839 by the Ulster Railway Company. It was rebuilt in 1878 to a design by William Henry Mills, for the newly formed Great Northern Railway Company (Ireland) GNR(I). Mills was chief civil engineer to the company from 1877 to 1909. The station is a fine example of the typical blueprint design, which was widely constructed on the system during the last quarter of the nineteenth century – a single-storey block in yellow brick with relieving and ornamental courses in brown, black and purple. The building was given a general 'face-lift' and 'tidy up' which resulted in it winning an award during European Architectural Heritage Year (1975). Maintenance is always a priority, much of the original ironwork is still in place. An elegant signal cabin, a fine example of GNR(I) architecture, once stood at Knockmore Junction. Built in 1887, again to designs by W.H. Mills, it was demolished in 1977.

Lisburn railway station, early 1900s. *(ILC & LM)*

Right: Knockmore signal cabin.

Far right: Lisburn railway station, 'southbound' platform. *(JSH)*

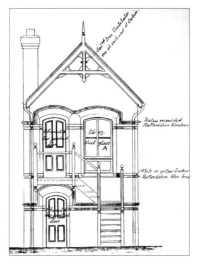

The Ulster Railway Company

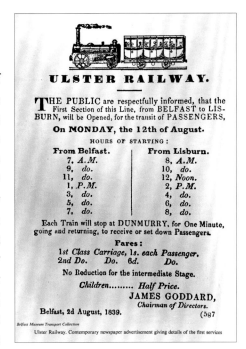

ULSTER RAILWAY.

THE PUBLIC are respectfully informed, that the First Section of this Line, from BELFAST to LISBURN, will be Opened, for the transit of PASSENGERS,

On MONDAY, the 12th of August.

HOURS OF STARTING:

From Belfast.	From Lisburn.
7, A.M.	8, A.M.
9, do.	10, do.
11, do.	12, Noon.
1, P.M.	2, P.M.
3, do.	4, do.
5, do.	6, do.
7, do.	8, do.

Each Train will stop at DUNMURRY, for One Minute, going and returning, to receive or set down Passengers.

Fares:

1st Class Carriage, 1s. each Passenger.
2nd Do. Do. 6d. Do.

No Reduction for the intermediate Stage.

Children......... Half Price.

JAMES GODDARD,
Chairman of Directors.

Belfast, 2d August, 1839. (587

Belfast Museum Transport Collection

Ulster Railway. Contemporary newspaper advertisement giving details of the first services

(ILC & LM)

THE ULSTER RAILWAY COMPANY was incorporated by Act of Parliament in 1836 with authority to construct a railway line linking Belfast with Armagh, a distance of thirty-six miles, and the first section of the Ulster Railway, the seven miles from Belfast to Lisburn was constructed between March 1837 and July 1839. The official opening of the line took place on Monday, 12 August 1839 when over three thousand people made the twenty minute journey from Belfast to Lisburn. There were seven trains daily in each direction, and the fare was one shilling in the first-class carriage, six pence in the second-class with children half price. There was only one intermediate station at Dunmurry, where the train stopped 'for one minute going and returning, to receive and set down passengers', but there was no reduction in the fare for using this in-between stage. McCutcheon writes in *The Industrial Archaeology of Northern Ireland*:

> Hundreds flocked to travel on the new line during its early days of operation, while many more lined the permanent way, flanked the cuttings and station platforms or crowded the parapets of the several bridges spanning the line.

Among those who went to see the first train coming into Lambeg was Richard Niven, Snr, who set out from Chrome Hill accompanied by his favourite dog, but sadly the dog was killed on that occasion. There were religious and environmental objections to the general introduction of railways. The Belfast Presbytery proclaimed that railways meant 'profanation of the Sabbath whereby vice and wickedness would increase.' Sir George Findlay recorded the objections that:

> The smoke of the engine would kill the birds, cattle would cease to give their milk. The sparks emitted would set fire to the houses and factories on the line of route; the race of the horses would become extinct, amidst which the absolute ruin of the country would shrink to the insignificance of a detail.

In the event the concerns were unfounded. Regular services were soon established on the single track and by 1841 there were six passenger trains in each direction on weekdays between Belfast and Lisburn, with three on Sundays, carrying approximately half a million people per annum. It had been the original decision of the Ulster Railway Board to run only first and second-class carriages, but the position was reviewed and in March 1840 third class travellers were accommodated as standing passengers in goods wagons. The numbers of third class passengers increased to such an extent that third class carriages were introduced, which had neither seats nor roofs, but were plain wagons, with sides 4ft 9in high, surmounted by a 6-inch high iron railing. In order to distinguish between the standing of the classes of passengers the third-class carriages were at first incorporated with goods wagons and run as a separate train, but by 1848 goods traffic had increased to such an extent that the open thirds were attached to passenger trains. The first and second-class carriages had roof seats for guards or police. The open thirds remained in use until 1856 when they were withdrawn following public reaction to an accident in which Patrick Flanagan was badly injured when he fell from an open carriage near Lisburn. In April 1885 the Royal Train carrying the Prince and Princess of Wales stopped in order that Sir Richard Wallace could meet his friends. The short visit was seen by large crowds of cheering Lisburn people.

The railway companies in Ireland had each developed their networks without having reached any agreement to conform to a standard gauge. By 1846 the Ulster Railway had constructed the Belfast – Portadown section of their railway at a gauge of 6ft 2in when an

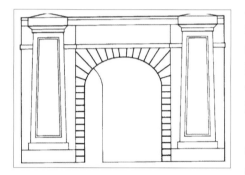

Act for Regulating the Gauge of Railways became law and established 5ft 3in as the gauge for railway construction in Ireland. The line up to this time had been single track and the stations had only one platform, but the bridges were fortunately double width and the change of gauge was started immediately. The conversion started by laying a new Up line to the new gauge, which was in use by the goods traffic in January 1847. From January to May the two gauges ran side by side while crossovers were put in at the stations to accommodate a mixed gauge at the platforms. Passenger trains with new rolling stock then diverted to the new Up line, while the original line was re-laid to the standard gauge. When this was completed the two lines operated as normal Up and Down lines.

Above: Design elevation for Ulster Railway's bridges at Lambeg.

Below: The underbridge at Glenmore, Lambeg. *(FGW)*

The railway network expanded in the second half of the nineteenth century and by 1876 the Ulster Railway Company and the other railway companies serving south and

southwest Ulster had amalgamated to form the Great Northern Railway. The 'Great Age of Steam' has long since passed and the new generation of diesel trains, which entered service on the line in 2005, are C3K trains, capable of speeds of up to 145 km/h, built by CAF at Zaragoza in northern Spain.

Travelling from Belfast, the rail approach to Lisburn crosses two Ulster Railway sandstone bridges at Lambeg, which McCutcheon describes as fine examples of early railway engineering. Built in red sandstone quarried near Moira and Magheralin, the soft, marly freestone lends itself to delicacy of expression in stone masonry. One bridge crosses the west entrance to Glenmore House, which is closed up and neglected. The second suffers visually from the official graffiti imposed by Road Service. The appearance of both could perhaps, be greatly enhanced by Council promoted clearing and planting.

The Temperance Institute

LISBURN TEMPERANCE INSTITUTE, NOW known as the Bridge Community Centre, is situated in Railway Street, on the periphery of the Lisburn Historic Quarter. Sir Richard Wallace, who died in 1890, the year the Institute was opened, donated the land on which the building was erected. The Lisburn Temperance Union was formed in 1887. The first president, James N. Richardson, a prominent local Quaker and a member of the family business of Richardson Sons and Owden, one of the largest bleachers in the Lagan valley area, contributed £800 towards a total building and furnishing cost of £3,500, and raised a further £800 from friends. John D.

Temperance Institute
(ILC & LM)

Barbour of Hilden, who was one of the first trustees, was also a large contributor to the building fund and his wife laid the foundation stone on 24 June 1889. The building, which was designed by the Belfast architects Young and Mackenzie, was built by Messrs D & P MacHenry.

The building fulfilled an objective of the Temperance Union by providing a suitable meeting place for townspeople and visitors; it created a Victorian community centre with recreation and meeting rooms, committee rooms, a billiard room, a reading room and library, and a café and kitchen. A suitably equipped gymnasium for boys and young men, offering classes for 'drill and callisthenics,' was built at the rear and stables were added at a later date. The Temperance Institute became the established popular venue for meetings of local clubs and associations and became an integral part of the social and business life of the community.

The building's usage changed with the times, stables became garages, the gymnasium became a billiard club, a badminton club, a table tennis club and was later converted to a ship for the Sea Cadets, membership of the library expanded and 4,500 volumes filled the bookcases before the Antrim County Library supplied the public need, and the café, which was a popular venue for lunches and functions, had graduated to wedding receptions before commercial pressures forced its closure. The building was an established feature of the Lisburn

Public drinking fountain in wall of Temperance Institute. *(JSH)*

Boot scraper, Railway Street. *(JSH)*

The Bridge Community
Centre, 2017.
(JSH)

townscape serving the needs of a growing community for over one hundred years by providing a base for a variety of clubs, groups and associations, which had been established by the citizens to meet current trends, interests or needs.

The responsibility for providing community facilities, similar to those available at the Temperance Institute, passed to Lisburn Borough Council in 1973 with the reorganisation of local government. The building was sold to the Borough Council in 1979 and opened as the Bridge Community Centre in 1981, providing a much needed and utilized service to the community. There was outrage amongst users when, in May 2003, a joint committee meeting of the Council recommended that users of the Bridge should be transferred to other council facilities and the premises be vacated by 2004. A Friends of the Bridge group was formed and officers elected who were tasked with organising a campaign to save The Bridge. The very public campaign resulted in the building being given listed status and a major refurbishment programme was implemented.

The Gymnasium, 2017
(JSH)

Looking back to 1969, Charles Brett and Lady Dunleath wrote in an Ulster Architectural Heritage Society publication; 'if the ratepayers of Lisburn choose….to allow their splendid heritage to decay, that is their right; but their children and grandchildren are unlikely to thank them for their short-sightedness.' We have made progress in the intervening years and the citizens of Lisburn now have a growing awareness and pride in their heritage, which was demonstrated by their support in saving the Bridge Community Centre.

County Antrim Infirmary

The County Antrim Infirmary was founded in the year 1767, and like all county infirmaries can trace its origin to an Act of the Irish Parliament passed in 1765. Lisburn's first hospital was formed following a meeting held in the home of the Bishop of Down and Connor. It was located in a house in Bow Lane, now Bow Street. The minutes of the Infirmary record that it was to open with eight beds for the use of patients, one for the housekeeper, one for the nurses and one for the porter, making eleven in all. The next entry refers to the provision of blankets from Thomas Wolfenden's blanket manufactory and records one of the earliest commitments to after sales service.

> 8 January 1767; Ordered that Mr Wolfenden be desired to make ten pairs of blankets as soon as possible. He promises at the same time that he would clean them at any time when desired, and without fee or reward.

Lisburn was fortunate to have such a hospital. Its object was to provide medicine for the poor of the Co. Antrim, both male and female, as well as providing medical or surgical aid. It was a much-needed institution and served the town and district well. In December 1773 the hospital committee accepted the offer of a larger house in 'an airy part of the town' belonging to Mr Edward Gayer, and this house in Seymour Street became the County Antrim Infirmary. A report stated its objective was to dispense medicines or advice, or both, to extern patients, or receive them as in-patients when they needed surgery. In the 1830s an average of 800 out-patients were treated annually with medication and 400 with medical advice; 290 were admitted for surgery or treatment.

County Antrim Infirmary, Seymour Street.
(ILC & LM)

One of the earliest surgeons was Dr. Dennis Kelly who died in 1777; another was Dr. Stewart, a well-known physician, who was succeeded by Dr. William Thompson, who occupied the post of surgeon for almost fifty years. The Thompson Memorial Home for Incurables was built by his relatives after his tragic death in 1882, when he was killed at Dunmurry crossing the railway. He was followed by Dr. George St. George. A successful general practitioner, Dr. St. George was connected to the County Antrim Infirmary for over fifty years and held the position of surgeon from 1882 until his death in 1922. For the greater part of that period his remuneration was a miserable £92 a year, but he was dedicated to his work there and was instrumental in making many improvements. He was also consulting surgeon to the Thompson Memorial Home. With the formation of Carson's Ulster Volunteer Force, he trained an ambulance class and following the outbreak of war he assisted and lectured to members of the Voluntary Aid Detachment. Lisburn had three V.A.D. units. Men and women from these units served with the forces in Europe. During the period of the war

209 sick and wounded soldiers were treated at the Infirmary and of this number there was only one death recorded. In recognition of his service the name of Dr. George St. George was included in a list of special mentions issued by the Secretary of State for War. In all aspects of his life his guiding principle was service to others.

The next occupant of the post was Lieutenant Colonel Dr. J.G. Johnston, who, during World War I, served with distinction with the 36th Ulster Division, 108th Field Ambulance, Royal Army Medical Corps. He had been a medical officer in the UVF and joined up

Dr. J.G. Johnston

(HK)

on the formation of the Ulster Division, serving at the Somme, Cambrai and St. Quentin. He was awarded the Military Cross in 1916, having been previously mentioned in despatches. He was appointed surgeon to the Infirmary and later also surgeon to the Lisburn and Hillsborough District Hospital (now the Lagan Valley Hospital). He held these appointments until the introduction of the National Health Service in 1948. He was President of the Northern Ireland Branch of the British Medical Association (B.M.A.) in 1948 and in 1951–52 President of the Ulster Medical Society as well as finding time to serve for periods on many other committees. In his address to the B.M.A. he outlined the history of county infirmaries and drew on his predecessor's 'interesting if lurid account' of the Infirmary in Seymour Street. This account is even more interesting when viewed with the benefit of our experience of present day standards of medical care and equipment.

The staff consisted of a Matron who was not a trained nurse, two nurses, neither of whom could either read or write and who had received no training whatsoever, and a porter. There was no night nursing at all. During the night one of the nurses occupied a bed in the female ward and the porter slept in one of the male wards. The Dispensary was the abode of very large black and grey slugs and cockroaches and the yard was infested with rats. There was one bathroom with the bath sunk in the stone-flagged floor and seldom if ever used. Behind the hospital were the pig-styes and a stream of sewerage flowed from these and found its way down the yard; flies were plentiful. The operating room had a wooden table and a wooden press which held the instruments. At each end of the room there was a human skeleton. In the wards there was no ventilation, except when the windows were open, which was very seldom. The beds were iron and the mattresses consisted of straw stuffed into ticks. The plates were wooden, and knives and forks weren't provided. There were no wash-basins or taps and vermin were plentiful, especially bugs. In 1882 there were forty operations performed, with four deaths, which was not too bad a result under the prevailing conditions.

In 1885, the first attempts at modernisation were made when extensive bathrooms and lavatory accommodation was provided. In 1887, a trained nurse was appointed as Matron and nurses were instituted in place of the attendants on the sick as previously. Also, in the same year, a change of mattresses from straw to wire-woven was a great advantage, rendering the wards cleaner and the air purer, as the debris of the straw when the beds were made floated about in the air. Thin hair mattresses over the wire ones were a better solution as the wire was cold to lie on in the winter. In 1893, it is reported that the amount of stimulants used during the year was four-and-a-half gallons of whiskey, thirty-nine dozen of stout and a gallon of gin. No wonder the surgeon and the place were popular! A horse ambulance was provided in 1896, by public subscription, for the removal of sick people and accident cases to the hospital. In 1904, electric light was provided by means of a petrol driven engine and dynamo, and the first X-ray plant was presented to the hospital by the Barbour family. This represented modern thinking. Only ten years previously, in 1895, X-rays had been first observed and documented by a German scientist, Wilhelm Conrad Rontgen who found them by accident when experimenting with vacuum tubes. He took an X-ray photograph of his wife's hand, which showed her wedding ring and her bones. The photograph generated great public and scientific interest in the new form of radiation. Rontgen called it 'X' to indicate it was an unknown type of radiation and the name stuck although (over Rontgen's objections) many of his colleagues suggested calling them Rontgen rays. The *Lisburn Standard* was referring to them as Rontgen rays in April 1922. The X-ray machine provided by Barbours was small, made a terrific noise and there was a visible spark of some 6–12 inches, which was enough to terrorise even the staff by this exhibition of internal thunder and lightning. William Barbour was a doctor by profession and practiced in the County Antrim Infirmary, Lisburn, before he went to America and settled in Quincy, Illinois.

In 1912, a new operating theatre and sterilising room were built, and an electric lift installed, and so, gradually, a comparatively modern hospital with most of the amenities for up-to-date treatment evolved from this primitive house of discomforts, insects and dirt.

The staff of the County Antrim Infirmary in the early 1900s. Dr. George St George MD and the Matron, Miss Melville, in the front row. *(ILC & LM)*

Lisburn Workhouse

UNDER THE PROVISIONS OF the 1838 Poor Law Act, Ireland was divided into 130 administrative units known as Poor Law Unions. Each had its own workhouse, which was administered by a Board of Guardians. These guardians of the poor, mostly landowners and businessmen, were authorised to erect a workhouse; to be responsible for its management and to levy rates for that purpose on the town of Lisburn and the twenty-six surrounding townlands. One Guardian represented each townland and there were three for Lisburn town. All were well-known men who performed their duties without payment.

The first meeting of the Board of Guardians was held in the Assembly Rooms, Market Square, on 20 February 1839, under the chairmanship of James Watson, of Brookhill. Mr. James Ward, of Lisburn, was appointed clerk at a salary of fifty pounds per annum. He had to obtain two sureties of fifty pounds each, and provide one of one hundred pounds himself. These guardians were hard-headed and tight-fisted. 'Every penny a prisoner' was their motto. There never was a penny spent that was not really needed for some purpose.

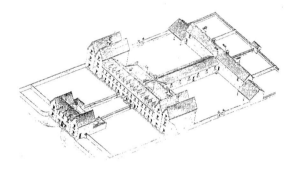

Architect's drawing of the workhouse.

The guardians asked the Marquess of Hertford to provide a building site of six acres for the workhouse and requested the Marquis of Downshire to supply free stone from his quarry near Moira for the building. A building committee met to consider plans for the workhouse and sought tenders from contractors. George Wilkinson, the Poor Law's official architect, advised that workhouses should be to a standard design, 'uniform, cheap, durable and unattractive'.

On 28 May 1839, the estimate of Arthur Williams and Sons, Dublin, was accepted at £6,200 and work commenced on a greenfield site on the Hillsborough Road. The workhouse was situated where the Lagan Valley Hospital now stands. The firm of Williams also built the workhouses at Lurgan and Belfast. During the famine years extra sleeping galleries for an additional 200 people were provided in the new workhouse.

An advertisement for a Workhouse Master, carried by the *Belfast Commercial Chronicle*, implied that a strict disciplinarian might be required to supervise the inmates: single men – 'persons who have served in the Army or Police, who are young and have good discharges will be preferred. Salary £40 per annum, with rations and apartments.' A Mr. McCartan was appointed to the post and sent to Lincoln Poorhouse for two or three weeks to learn the system and prepare for the rush. This was necessary, for within a week of opening, on 11 February 1841, 250 paupers, old, young or infirm, were admitted to straw mattressed beds. There was a padded cell for 'lunatics', the term then in use. On arrival the inmates were given a bath and their clothes were replaced. An order for clothing for 250 to

400 suits for men and boys and the same for women and girls had been placed. A stock of clogs had been laid in, each pair costing 4s 4d for a man and 3s 6d for a woman, and each pauper was given a pair.

During the Famine of 1843–1848, potatoes, which were the staple diet for the inmates, were no longer available and were replaced with a diet of oatmeal, buttermilk, rice, a soup made from cows' or sheep's heads, and bread. The famine continued and the contractor for the supply of potatoes asked to be released from his contract. At a meeting of the guardians in April 1843, the estimate of provisions required for the ensuing week was: 1 ton oatmeal, 117 lbs bread, 2,600 quarts buttermilk, 210 quarts sweet milk, 2 lbs butter, 26 lbs beef – cows' and sheep's heads, 1 lb tea, 4 lbs sugar, 2 lbs salt, 2 lbs pepper. Total in workhouse 525, total in hospital 52. The average cost of a pauper for the week was eleven pence. No mention of potatoes.

On his one and only visit to Lisburn in 1845 the 4th Marquess of Hertford visited the workhouse. He was pleased with all that he saw and said that it was not excelled by any similar institution in England. He ordered a good dinner be provided for the paupers at his expense consisting of beef, carrots and soup, followed by tea and buns. In Sir Richard Wallace's time the prominent Quaker, James N. Richardson of Lissue, entertained the inmates to a selection of fruit and sweetmeats, annually, on New Year's Day,

In 1852, the *Greenock Advertiser* recorded the findings of a visitor from Scotland, who, on a mission to examine the system for the management of pauperism in Ireland, called at Lisburn. He met with the Workhouse Master, a Mr McKie, a gentleman of Scotch descent and of the Methodist persuasion, who conducted him around the house.

The house is of very tasteful architecture with long avenues and spaces of ground on

The Lagan Valley Hospital, 2017.
(JSH)

all sides blooming with vegetation. Nothing could exceed the milk-white cleanliness of the floors, walls, doors and other furniture of the establishment. There are fifteen acres of ground attached to it, which are kept in excellent state of cultivation by the master, without any assistance but the paupers. He preserves the manure derived from the house and scatters it over the soil, the liquid portion of it by means of pipes of his own manufacture. When the workhouse contained 952 inmates, during the Irish famine, the paid functionaries were eight in number, consisting of himself at £50 per annum, his wife at £25, an assistant master, who acted as clerk at £15, a schoolmaster at £20, a schoolmistress at £15, a porter at £11 10s, a tailor at £12, and a shoemaker at £12. These had their bed and board in addition.

The inmates were engaged in educational and industrial occupations. There was a bakery, shoemaking, tailoring, weaving, smith-work and joinery work for the men and boys and for the women and girls knitting, sewing, washing and dressing. In August 1843, broken stones were being sold at 1s 6d a ton to Ralph Jefferson for use on the Mail Coach Road (now the Belfast Road). The finances for the Lisburn Union appear to have been well managed. The poor rates increased during the famine years, the Union paid £5,000 of rate-in-aid for the distressed unions in the west of Ireland, paid £800 a year towards reducing the poor-house debt and still had £3,000 in the bank. The Lisburn Poor Law Union had survived the famine years, if purely in financial terms, with relatively little hardship.

By 1895, this glowing review had faded somewhat, according to a report for the *British Medical Journal* which condemned cramped wards, insanitary conditions, poor ventilation and heating:

> The whole system, in so far as it affects the aged, the lunatics, and the infants, requires humanising and the wants of each class need to be considered and provided for, for at present these classes appear to have been overlooked.

The Lisburn Workhouse, under the management of the Board of Guardians, carried on from 1840 in good times and bad, until the necessity of finding a home for the destitute became a thing of the past. In the 1901 census there were 223 inmates in the workhouse. On 22 April 1922 the workhouse, with a capacity of 1,000 persons, was empty, the last remaining eighty inmates had been housed in Lurgan. A section of the stone building became the core of the new Lisburn and Hillsborough District Hospital, which in 1947 became the Lagan Valley Hospital.

The Harp Society – The Egan Harp

The Harp Society was founded in Belfast, on St. Patrick's Day 1808, by some members of the Belfast Society for Promoting Knowledge with the aim of 'preserving the National Music and National Instrument of Ireland by instructing a number of blind children in playing the Irish Harp and also for procuring and disseminating information relative to the language, history and antiquities of Ireland.' Henry Bell of Lambeg was one of the original subscribers to the society and it was on his recommendation that fourteen-year-old Patrick McGrath from Dundalk, Co. Louth, was enrolled as a pupil. Arthur O'Neill, the blind seventy-five-year-old harper from Co. Tyrone, was appointed instructor to the society, which had twelve blind pupils, one of whom was a female, Bridget O'Reilly from Co. Cavan. By 1812 the society was in severe financial difficulties and the school was forced to close in the following year.

When news of these difficulties reached John Williamson Fulton in India, through the pages of the *Belfast Commercial Chronicle,* he raised a subscription to enable the Harp Society to continue. He collected a sum exceeding £1,192, principally from Irishmen residing in India, many of them officers in the army, and remitted the money to Mr Henry Joy of Belfast, and Mr Robert Williamson of Lambeg. This generous funding revived the society, which continued for a further twenty years. Henry Bell, writing in 1853, had this to say about the work of the society:

> To the munificent exertions of this society, Ireland is indebted for the preservation and continuance, in the present day, of her national instrument, which otherwise must have long since sunk for ever into silence. …Had this interesting object then been suffered to fall into neglect, our national airs, which are now frequently performed at the Courts of Balmoral and Windsor, by a pupil of this society, Pat Byrne, the 'Queen's Irish Harper,' these airs would not in the present day, thus aid in keeping alive in the good heart of our gracious Queen Victoria, those noble sympathetic feelings of interest in old Ireland.

The Irish Harp Society erected a headstone in Kilrush graveyard, Lisburn, to the memory of another of their pupils, Patrick McCloskey, 'in consideration of his good conduct and proficiency in music', who died 7 June 1826, aged 19 years. The stone no longer exists. Patrick McCloskey would have remained with the Harp Society as a pupil for only two years, and died as a practising harper; but as Aiken McClelland points out, 'his tombstone testifies to the interest maintained by members of the Society in their ex-pupils.' Were those members of the society Henry Bell and Robert Williamson?

John Egan was a noted Irish harp maker working in Dublin from circa 1804 to 1841. Regarded as Dublin's leading harp maker at the time, he made more than two thousand harps, from small Irish harps with blades to double-action pedal harps. He made the

Miss Maud J.G. Hunter (1860–1951). *(ILC & LM)*

The restored Egan Harp.
(ILC & LM)

instruments for the Belfast Harp Festival. The Egan family name was synonymous with harps and harp music. John's brother Charles Egan composed works for the instrument and their nephew, Francis Hewson, was also making pedal harps in the 1840s. There are Egan harps to be found in major collections worldwide including the Smithsonian Museum, Boston College, Cambridge University, the Victoria and Albert Museum and the National Museum of Ireland.

Mr F.S. Napier graciously donated an Egan harp to Lisburn Museum in 2002 and through a generous grant from the Heritage Lottery Fund it was fully restored to its playable state, almost two hundred years after its construction. The harp was last in the ownership of and played by Miss Maud J. G. Hunter (1860–1951), a concert harpist and piano and harp teacher in Lisburn. Miss Hunter was the organist at Seymour Street Methodist Church for more than thirty years. At church 'socials' she accompanied invited artistes on the harp.

The newly restored harp was first unveiled, to an invited audience, in the setting of Lisburn's Assembly Room at a recital and talk on late eighteenth century single-action harp music, given by Danielle Perrett, the established solo harpist and chamber music player. It was appropriate that Ms Perrett's opening selection featured her own arrangements of Irish melodies; Turlough O'Carolan's *Planxty Drury, Bumper Squire Jones, Grace Nugent, Mrs Crofton* and *Carolan's Concerto* as well as ancient Irish melodies by Charles Egan. *The Coolin* and *Ballinderry,* arranged by Bunting (1840) and *Na Geanna Fiaine* and *Three Sea Captains*, arranged by Grainne Yeats (20th Century) continued the Celtic theme. The range of the instrument was demonstrated after an interval with Sonatas by P.J. Hinner (1754–1805), J.B. Krumpholtz (1745–1790) and Mme. Dussek (1775–1847) and Charles Egan's French air paired with Petrini's variations on *La Bonne Aventure O Gué.*

Portrait of an Artist and his Wife by Nicholas J. Crowley (1819–1857).
(RWP Private Collection)

In the Regency era, as in the novels of Jane Austen, harp music filled the drawing rooms of London, Dublin and the great country houses. Aristocratic ladies like the Duchess of Richmond played Egan harps, and by 1821 Egan was 'Harp Maker to His Majesty George IV.'

The harp, one of the national symbols of Ireland, has traditionally been regarded as the instrument of aristocratic society and a painting *Portrait of an Artist and his Wife,* attributed to the Dublin born artist Nicholas Joseph Crowley (1819–1857), captures all the warmth and splendour of a grand interior.

Captain Nickerson's Watch

EARLY IN 2017, A watch, formerly the property of Captain Moses Nickerson, was acquired by Lisburn Museum from an auction house in America. The watch was described as a:

> … historically important men's gold fuseé pocket watch with eleven jewels, key wind and set, gilt full plate movement with lever escapement in an 18 carat, yellow gold, engine-turned and engraved consular open face case with London hallmark and date letter for the year 1857. It has a Roman numeral gold dial, with blued steel fleur de lys style hands. It was made by Gilbert and Sons, Belfast. It was sold with a 14-carat gold chain, and two keys.

The reason for this important purchase was the close historical connection of this watch with the sufferings of the cotton weavers from the Maze, Broomhedge and Lisburn areas in 1863–64. Who was Captain Moses Nickerson? He was born in Chatham, Massachusetts in 1812 and was an experienced Master Mariner having led several whaling expeditions. His cousin Thomas Nickerson, also a captain, was stranded at sea for three months after his ship was sunk by a whale. His story inspired Herman Melville's book, *Moby Dick*. Moses Nickerson died at sea in 1871 while sailing between Sicily and Boston.

Captain Moses Nickerson, aged 34, by Charles Cohill (c.1812–c.1860)
(Image courtesy of Joshua F. Eldred, President of Eldreds Auctions, MA, USA)

The American Civil War began in 1861 and by the spring of the following year large areas of the cotton fields in the southern states were left untilled and lying barren. This led to a serious reduction in the imports of cotton into the mills in England and Scotland, which led to unemployment and suffering particularly among the weavers and their families. These effects were also felt among those in the industry in Ulster. The wider Lisburn area, prior to the growth in the linen industry, was particularly badly affected. There were alarming reports of destitution and deprivation in the area during Christmas week 1862. Many people had been employed producing immense quantities of muslin for the mills of the Glasgow manufacturers. During the Christmas holidays of that year, David Carlisle of the Maze and Hugh McCall of Lisburn carried out inspections and found there was severe poverty and starvation among the weaver population. They petitioned the Lisburn town commissioners and as a result a meeting was held in the Court House on the 8 January 1863. Among those who spoke at the meeting were Hugh McCall and the Rev. E. Franks, a Wesleyan minister stationed at the Maze.

Mr. Hugh McCall reported that within a circle of ten or twelve miles around Lisburn, there existed a greater number of hand-loom weavers than could be found in either Manchester, Bolton or Glasgow, but the wages earned by Irish weavers, even in the best times, were far below those earned by their English or Scottish counterparts. No other class

Mr. Hugh McCall

of workmen in the kingdom were so easily pleased in the matter of wages as the weavers of the north of Ireland. Their wants were few and their habits simple; indeed, a state of things which an English operative could only look upon as that of sheer poverty could be considered by an Ulster hand-loom weaver as a condition of comparative comfort.

Rev. E. Franks addressed the meeting at some length on the scenes of distress which had come under his own notice, and which he depicted with such graphic power as to elect the entire sympathy of every person present. He spoke of the cotton weavers of the district as a class of highly moral men and second to none with whom he had ever before come in contact. He said that the people of the Maze were those of which any nation might well be proud. The meeting did a lot to provide effective assistance. A subscription list was set up and a committee was created to organise relief. Advertisements were published in the Belfast newspapers looking for donations of Indian meal, oatmeal, and coal. Blankets were ordered from a Yorkshire manufacturer. A Ladies' Convention was established which met twice a week and arranged the purchase of clothing, the making of underclothing, sheets, blankets, frocks for girls and children, and their distribution among the female section of the cotton weavers. The committee sent letters soliciting aid to the Marquess of Hertford, (who did not respond) and manufacturers and merchants in Belfast, Liverpool, Scotland, New York, Philadelphia, Montreal, Ottawa and Toronto. Letters and reports were published in the *Liverpool Daily Post, Belfast News Letter, Northern Whig* and *The Times*. The appeals for support and finance by the committee were successful, and gifts of food, clothing, services and money were received both from home and abroad. The winter was severe and the claims on the relief fund increased, but the aid given to the poor households never exceeded one shilling worth of meal and coal to each member of the family, and this enabled large numbers to be supported.

The relief committee were asked by a deputation of weavers to try to arrange for some of them to emigrate to the colonies. As a result, the ship *Old Hickory*, which had arrived with a cargo of flour for the distressed – the gift of Philadelphia – was fitted out with berths and sailed on the return journey with 253 passengers on the 27 May 1863. The *News Letter* gave a moving account of the weavers and their families accompanied by an immense number of neighbours and friends passing through Lisburn to the railway station, where they departed for Belfast. Here they were transported on carts and lorries to the quay. Their departure attracted a crowd of between 3,000 and 4,000 well-wishers to see them off.

In May 1863, the greatly depleted relief fund was given a major boost when Alex. T. Stewart, originally from Lissue, sent the barque *Mary Edson* to Belfast with a cargo of bread stuffs and provisions valued at over £3,000. The *Mary Edson* was built in 1859. Mr Stewart had also chartered the vessel for the return trip to transport distressed weavers and their families to America. While the vessel was docked in Belfast, carpenters and other workmen created suitable accommodation for the passage to New York. The ship arrived there on 1 August 1863. Such was the number of applicants for free passage, the task of selection was difficult and the *Mary Edson*, with 137 adults and children aboard, sailed from Belfast quay in July 1863.

This is where the watch enters the story. Moses Nickerson, the Captain of the *Mary Edson*, was presented with the watch as the ship was about to sail from Belfast. The commemorative gold watch is engraved with the following inscription:

Presented by the Lisburn Relief Committee and Others, to Captain Nickerson of the Barque Mary Edson, the good ship that bore across the Atlantic the noble gift bestowed on his suffering countrymen by A.T. Stewart, Esq., of New York, July 1863.

Later in the year conditions began to improve and the amount of relief required was much less, but many families still required assistance due to ill health and bodily weakness. The sufferings which had been endured in the early part of the year still took their toll. In the country districts much distress still existed, for, although the demand for weaving had improved, the rate of wages continued so low that the best hands at the loom could not earn an adequate wage. The work of the Relief Committee was wound down at the end of 1863 after an effective and successful operation. Just over 150 years later, the gold watch, a symbol of what became known as the Cotton Famine, is an important exhibit in Lisburn Museum.

Gold fuseé pocket watch presented to Captain Nickerson, Captain of the barque *Mary Edson*.
(ILC & LM)

Barque *Mary Edson* off the White Cliffs of Dover.
(Photograph courtesy of C.L. Prichett Antiques.)

Sir Robert Hart

Sir Robert Hart by Frank McKelvey.
(Naughton Gallery QUB)

ROBERT HART, THE ELDEST son of Henry Hart and Ann Edgar, was born 20 February 1835 at Woodhouse Street, Portadown. The Harts, a middle-class Ulster family with a background in distilling, shop-keeping and farming, moved from Portadown to Ravarnette House, outside Lisburn. Robert was sent to the Wesleyan school at Taunton, Somerset, but his father's anger at him being allowed to return home unaccompanied at the end of the school year led him to be sent to the Wesley Connexional School, Dublin, instead. Hart, aged 15 years, entered the newly founded Queen's College, Belfast, where he distinguished himself by obtaining a scholarship for each academic year. He graduated with a Bachelor of Arts in 1853 when he was 18 years old. He was the only candidate awarded a graduate scholarship in Modern Languages. In the spring of 1854 Hart was nominated by Queen's College for the Consular Service in China. He was appointed to the post of Supernumerary Interpreter in China. With £100 for his passage, Robert Hart set sail for China. He was 19 years old.

Hart spent his first three months in Hong Kong as a Student Interpreter and was then appointed to the British Consulate at Ningpo, where he remained until March 1858. From Ningpo he moved on to Canton, initially as secretary to the Allied Commission (responsible for governing the city) and then in October as interpreter at the British Consulate there.

In May 1859, Robert Hart resigned from the British Consular Service. The Canton Viceroy, Laou Tsung Kwang asked him to join the Chinese Imperial Maritime Customs (CIMC). He was appointed Deputy-Commissioner at Canton.

In 1861, H.N. Lay, the Inspector General of the CIMC, returned to England on leave for two years. Robert Hart was appointed an Officiating Inspector-General during this time. This gave Hart an opportunity to expand his experience and show his ability. When Lay returned in May 1863 Hart was made Commissioner at Shanghai, with responsibility for the Yangtsze ports. This post was created for Hart by Prince Kung.

In the post of Inspector-General of the CIMC Hart was responsible to the Chinese government for the operating of the multinational Customs Service. He wielded enormous power, often negotiating with American and European authorities, all with major interests in China. By the end of the 19th century the Customs Service was responsible for the Chinese Imperial Postal Service, port development, inland and coastal waterways, as well as collecting revenue. Hart's main responsibilities included collecting custom duties, as well as expanding the new system to more sea and river ports

'Chinese Customs' original drawing by Imp for *Vanity Fair* 27 December 1894.

and some inland frontiers, standardising its operations, and insisting on exacting standards of efficiency and honesty. The CIMC was operating in seven ports in 1863 when Hart became Inspector-General; by 1907 it was operating in seventy-six native customs stations under his authority. He presided over the servicing of 182 lights, various navigational aids, and 2,800 post offices. His staff numbered 11,970 of whom 1,345 were foreigners. Hart worked to persuade China to establish its own embassies in foreign countries.

In 1857, Hart took a Chinese concubine, Ayaou, with whom he had three children and for whom he developed genuine affection and respect. After becoming Inspector General one of his resolutions was to set a good example to his staff. For him this included parting with Ayaou and finding a respectable British wife. After twelve years in China, Hart returned home on leave in May 1866 and whilst on leave he met and married Hester (Hessie) Jane Bredon, also from Portadown. She was nineteen years old. After a hurried courtship they married on 22 August 1866 in St Thomas Parish Church, Dublin. Following a brief honeymoon in Killarney the couple sailed for China. Hessie remained in China until March 1876, when she returned to Europe with their two children – a daughter, Evelyn Amy and a son, Edgar Bruce. Hart was reunited with his family when he travelled to Paris for the Exposition Universelle de 1878, as President of the Chinese Commission. The family returned to China in Spring 1879. Hart's second daughter, Mabel Milburne was born in November that year. Hart settled back into family life in Peking and moved into a new residence. In 1882, Hessie and the children returned to Europe – this time for good – the relationship was maintained by letter. Robert Hart was not to see his wife again until she came to visit in 1906, when they spent three months in Peking. In a letter to Campbell, his agent in London, Hart wrote:

The Candlelabra

> It is, of course, pleasant to have wife and daughter here, but, after two dozen years of solitariness, I don't run as easily in 'double harness' as I would have done had I been at it all the time!

The Tureen

Hart received international recognition for his work and was awarded many honours in the course of his career, some of which include Chevalier of the Order of Vasa (1870), Sweden; the Peacock's Feather, (1885), China; the Ancestral Rank of the First Class of the First Order for Three Generations, (1889), China; Baronet, (1893), Great Britain; Knight Commander of the Order of Pius IX, Holy See, (1885); Knight Grand Cross of the Order of Orange Nassau, (1897); First Class of the Order of St Anna, (1907), Russia. In 1901, in recognition of his services in connection with the peace negotiations, the Emperor bestowed the title of Brevet Junior Guardian to the Heir-Apparent, a title awarded to Li Hung Chang and Prince Ching for the same service – it had never before been conferred on a foreigner. Weighted with the ribbons and awards of success, we get a glimpse of a reflective, isolated and rather lonely Robert Hart writing home in July 1889, in response to a local Methodist church appeal:

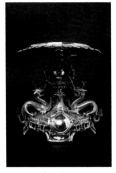

The Comportiere

Table silver given to Sir Robert Hart in 1908 by the Chinese Empress Dowager to mark his retirement.
(Naughton Gallery QUB)

Hart memorial, Blaris
Old Burial Ground.

Sir Robert Hart's grave
All Saint's Church,
Bisham, Berkshire.

Mandarin Chinese plaque on the
Hart memorial. (JSH)

I am glad you thought of writing to me in connection with the Zion Jubilee, for, long as it is since I left that part of the world, I still have an affectionate recollection of the place and people. … I can see down the hill, and over the bridge, and away along the broad straight road, with tall trees on each side, having on one hand Carlisle's house, and on the other the lane that led up to Sam Jones', and which, after passing the Phenix's and Bradbury's, touches the Maze and turns off by Knox's; indeed, as I write, it is astonishing how forty years ago comes back again! I suppose it is the same for all who go far from home and work in foreign lands: we never forget, and a sound, or a smell, or a sight brings up cradle-days, and all the dear surroundings of Home Sweet Home. I have had to stop here for a moment; the tears fill into my eyes – fancy weeping in '89 in Peking, over recollections in Priesthill in '49 but so it is, and it is good to have one's memory roused and one's heart touched and wakened from the loneliness and worldliness of age.

Hart applied for leave of absence in 1908 and returned to England. His world contribution was recognised by various presentations. He was Pro-Chancellor of Queen's University from 1908–1911. Sir Robert was entertained in Lisburn Town Hall by members of the Urban Council, who recognised his early associations with the town and presented him with an address. In his reply Sir Robert recalled that it was almost seventy years ago that he first became acquainted with the town and it was more than thirty years since he walked through the streets. He had a vivid recollection of it and its vicinity, as he told them:

It was here at Timothy O'Loughlin's my first pony saddle was made in the early 'forties' and it was also here in the early 'fifties' that I read my last Latin with Mr Patterson, before entering Queen's College, Belfast … and if I recall the stirring scenes of the Tuesday market and fair days, it is to let you see that Lisburn has always had a warm place in my memory.

Sir Robert Hart died on 20 September 1911. He is buried at All Saint's Church in Bisham, near Marlow, in Berkshire. Recently a group of interested people came together to refurbish his burial place.

Alexander Turney Stewart

ALEXANDER TURNEY STEWART WAS born in 1803 at Lissue outside Lisburn, the son of Alexander Stewart and Margaret Stewart née Turney. Stewart was descended from both Scottish and Huguenot ancestors. His father died shortly before Stewart's birth and his mother remarried and emigrated to America the following year, leaving the infant Stewart in the care of his grandfather, John Turney. When his grandfather died he was taken in by Thomas Lamb, a Quaker who lived at Peartree Hill outside Lisburn. Young Stewart was educated at Belfast Academical Institution.

Alexander Turney Stewart

In 1818, A.T. Stewart sailed for America and found employment as a tutor in New York. He returned to Ireland in 1823, apparently to collect an inheritance from his grandfather's estate. He purchased a supply of linens and laces which he took back to New York and opened his first store on Broadway. Shortly afterward he married Cornelia Mitchell Clinch, daughter of a wealthy ship chandler. He rented a small shop at 283, Broadway, and the *New York Daily Advertiser* of 2 September 1823 carried this advertisement:

> A.T. Stewart, just arrived from Belfast, offers for sale to the Ladies of New York a choice selection of Fresh Dry Goods at Two Hundred Eighty-three Broadway.

This direct appeal to 'Ladies' was the first hint of Stewart's merchandising genius. In a year he had outgrown this shop and moved to larger premises. These proved too small and he was on the move again. This third shop was the first in America to have full length mirrors and Stewart invited the ladies of New York to come and see themselves as others see them. Stewart had a natural flair for marketing. He was the first in New York to promote the 'Cost Price' sale. In 1830 he advertised:

> Mr. A.T. Stewart, having purchased a large amount of goods soon to arrive, is obliged, in order to make room for these, to dispose of all stock he has on hand, which will be sold at Actual Cost, beginning Monday at eight a.m. Ladies are requested to come early to avoid the crush.

He also ran 'Fire Sales' although he never had a fire in his property. Another of his ploys was a ten per cent discount for school teachers and clergymen: this ten per cent, supposedly his profit, also applied to their family members.

It was said by one of his cashiers that 'over half of the people in New York are clergymen or teachers.' He introduced a policy of one retail price for all customers and accepted returned goods for exchange or cash. Later in his career he introduced the 'Remnant Sale' where the unsuspecting customer thought she was buying the remnant of a web of towelling or dress material, but these were prepared 'Remnants,' previously cut and prepared by Stewart's staff in lengths of a kind and quality that would appeal to the average

New York City residence of A.T. Stewart, corner of 3rd Street and 5th Avenue.

Stewart's retail store at Broadway and 10th Street, New York.

purchaser. The remnant was marked at the sale price – no bidding, no haggling – the recipe for a quick sale.

As his business continued to grow rapidly he had of necessity to move to bigger and bigger premises. His retail premises catered to wealthy New York women, while his wholesale department serviced the rest of the country. In 1876, he entered the mail order business. In 1846, he opened a retail emporium faced in marble, which became known as his Marble Palace. Stewart's innovative store became a thriving business as well as an attraction for visitors to New York. The store's gleaming white marble set it apart in a city of brick and brownstone. A *Guidebook to New York*, published in 1869, said Stewart's Marble Palace was 'the admiration of the town and wonder of the country, and so distinctive that the proprietor has never put up a sign.' In 1862, his new store development on Broadway, the six storey Iron Palace was the largest retail store in the world.

During the American Civil War he was very active in his support for the Union cause, working with the Union Defence Committee providing many of the supplies for General

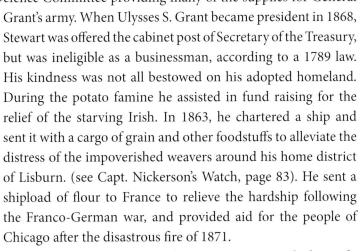

Grant's army. When Ulysses S. Grant became president in 1868, Stewart was offered the cabinet post of Secretary of the Treasury, but was ineligible as a businessman, according to a 1789 law. His kindness was not all bestowed on his adopted homeland. During the potato famine he assisted in fund raising for the relief of the starving Irish. In 1863, he chartered a ship and sent it with a cargo of grain and other foodstuffs to alleviate the distress of the impoverished weavers around his home district of Lisburn. (see Capt. Nickerson's Watch, page 83). He sent a shipload of flour to France to relieve the hardship following the Franco-German war, and provided aid for the people of Chicago after the disastrous fire of 1871.

By now he was the third richest man in New York alongside Cornelius Vanderbilt and William B. Astor, worth an estimated $40 million. However, both of these gentlemen had inherited their fortune and invested in property, whereas Stewart had made his money in the retail trade during his lifetime. A.T. Stewart, known as 'the Merchant Prince', for his successful

A.T. Stewart.
(ILC & LM)

development of his department stores had also grand ideas in terms of property development. He purchased 7,000 acres on Long Island and began to build a model Garden City at Hempstead Plains. His plans included attractive houses, wide streets, a waterworks, a hotel and a railroad connection to New York City. Stewart's business interests continued to thrive and he employed thousands of workers. At his death on 10 April 1876 he owned wholesale and retail stores, stocks, interests in New England, New York and New Jersey, mills, offices and warehouses in England, Ireland, Scotland, France, Germany and Switzerland and in New York he owned the Grand Union Hotel, Metropolitan Hotel, the Globe Theatre and Niblo's Garden, all well-known landmarks of the time.

His wife, Cornelia, continued with his plans and funded the building of the Episcopal Cathedral in Garden City as a memorial to her husband. However, he was not allowed to rest in peace. His coffin was stolen from the family vault and a large ransom was paid by his wife for its return. Eventually he was laid to rest in the crypt of his cathedral, the Cathedral of the Incarnation, which opened its doors on 9 April 1885. Today a bust of A.T. Stewart by Granville W. Carter, the cathedral and Stewart Avenue running through Garden City, are the main reminders of a young Lisburn immigrant who became one of the richest men in America.

John Ballance

John Ballance was born on 27 March 1839, the eldest son of Samuel and Mary Ballance née McNeice of Ballypitmave, near Glenavy, Co. Antrim. His father was a Protestant tenant farmer 'with evangelical tendencies'; his mother was a Quaker from a prominent local family. John Ballance was educated at the local national school and at Wilson's Academy in Belfast. He left the Academy before completing his education and took a job with a Belfast hardware firm. In 1857, he left Belfast for Birmingham, where he worked as a travelling salesman and attended evening classes to improve his position and prospects.

(JSH)

John Ballance, Prime Minister of New Zealand. (1891–1893).
(Philip Tennyson Cole 'Portrait of the Right Honourable John Ballance' 1893, watercolour on paper, 1936/1/1. Collection of the Sarjeant Gallery Te Whare o Rehua Whanganui. Bequest of Ellen Ballance, 1936.)

While in Birmingham he met Fanny Taylor and they were married in St. Peter and St. Paul's Church, Acton. He was aged 24. Fanny suffered poor health, and this encouraged the couple to travel to New Zealand in the hope that the warmer climate would be of benefit to her. They settled in Wanganui, North Island, and were unsuccessful in business ventures in sheep-farming and retail jewellery. He moved into journalism and in 1867 founded and edited the *Evening Herald*, which in 1876 became the *Wanganui Herald*. He owned it until his death, editing it whenever his later parliamentary duties permitted. Sadly, his wife died in 1868, aged 24. In May 1870 he married Ellen Anderson (d.1930), the daughter of an English army officer, born in Co. Down. They had two adopted children.

Ballance statue in
Wellington.

John Ballance put his name forward as a candidate in the 1873 elections for
the House of Representatives but withdrew before the vote. When he was elected
in 1875 he made his reputation in the spheres of the economy and land use. He
held office in different administrations: as colonial treasurer (1878), as minister for
lands and native affairs (1884–7). He also held the defence portfolio, fortified New
Zealand's ports and formed a permanent militia. He was re-elected (1887, 1890);
became leader of the opposition in 1889 and after a hard-fought election in 1891, he
replaced his former colleague, Sir Harry Atkinson, as Prime Minister. Ballance was
a Liberal and a champion of Maori issues. He was also a leading advocate of female
suffrage; in 1890, he told the New Zealand Parliament 'I believe in the absolute
equality of the sexes and I think they should be in the enjoyment of equal privileges in
political matters'. In fact, inspired by Ballance's stance, and shortly after his death, New
Zealand became the first country to give women the vote.

Ballance's health caused problems during the two years of his premiership and he died
of cancer on 27 April 1893. He was given a State Funeral and buried under an Irish granite
headstone in Wanganui. His statue stands in the Parliament grounds in Wellington. His
birthplace, outside Lisburn, has been restored by the Ulster New Zealand Trust and is open
to the public. John Ballance was acknowledged to be a man of great honesty and integrity,
gaining for himself the sobriquet 'the Rainmaker' for his ability to bring about prosperity,
and earned lasting respect as a reforming, enlightened and accomplished politician.

The John Ballance
statue in Wanganui,
New Zealand.

Above: Ballance House, Glenavy.
Headquarters of the Ulster New
Zealand Trust. *(JSH)*

Ballance House is home to the New Zealand
Consulate in Northern Ireland. *(JSH)*

Samuel McCloy

Samuel McCloy
(ILC & LM)

SAMUEL MCCLOY WAS BORN in Lisburn on 13 March 1831, the youngest of five children of Peter McCloy, painter and glazier of Bridge Street, and Martha Pelan. His parents were married in First Lisburn Presbyterian Church on 19 February 1823. The McCloy family's connections with Lisburn are long established, stretching back to the late eighteenth century. McCloy began his artistic career when he was apprenticed to a firm of his relatives J. & T. Smyth, a firm of engravers and lithographers in Castle Street, Belfast. In the fifth year of his apprenticeship he was admitted to the old Belfast Government School of Design, where he gained an exhibition and several prizes. He must have shown great promise as he was one of three pupils sent to the Training School for Masters at South Kensington, London, and in the spring of 1854 he was appointed Master of the Waterford School of Art. This was one of twenty-one provincial Schools of Design established throughout the British Isles by the Board of Trade with the aim of turning out skilled designers for industry, rather than painters and sculptors. He probably received a salary of around £140: bearing in mind that he was the only teacher in the school and taught both morning and evening classes, this was a meagre salary. Despite his duties McCloy still found time to paint and sent a number of his paintings to exhibitions in Dublin and London. He held this post for several years and exhibited at the Royal Hibernian Academy, Dublin, in 1862, 1870 and 1874, and at the Royal Society of British Artists. His works were also accepted from time to time by the Royal Academy, and it is reported that one of these, an Irish subject with many figures, was bought by Sir Richard Wallace by whom it was sent to the highly successful Industrial Exhibition, held in the Ulster Hall in 1876. McCloy had eleven works on display in this exhibition, which sold well.

In 1865, he married one of his pupils, the twenty-year-old Ellen Lucy Harris, who bore him nine children, six daughters and three sons. Around 1874 the family left Waterford and moved to Belfast, where they lived first at 9 Magdala Street, a large three-story house near the University and then for some reason moved to No. 11, the house next door. Although he continued to paint, McCloy's main income was from illustrations done for Marcus Ward, a well-known Belfast publishing firm. He also painted figures for illuminated addresses, and designed Christmas and greetings cards. He made drawings on wood and other work: Marcus Ward employed wood carvers at that time. He also made several designs for damask tablecloths for a local firm, John Shaw Brown and Sons, but he gave this up as he found the technicalities irksome and uninteresting. Several of his designs were woven. McCloy also produced many watercolours for a commercial art gallery in Pall Mall, London. These were mostly single-figure subjects. According to family tradition he worked as an illustrator for the *Illustrated London News*. He continued to exhibit at the Royal Hibernian Academy until 1884. He remained in Belfast until 1881 according to Strickland, but according to family sources the move to London took place in 1884, having lived for a short time in Bangor. When his uncle died and left him a property at 47 Solon New Road, Clapham, the family moved to London. This was a sensible decision enabling him to sell his work through the London galleries. He exhibited little during the London period; once at the Royal Institution and a few times at the Royal Society of British Artists. He was a friendly and jovial man who enjoyed playing games with his children and he often used them as models, bribing them to sit for hours with offers of a penny or half penny reward. A staunch Presbyterian, he was proud of his Ulster ancestry and the fact that he could trace his family back to the Siege of Derry.

Algernon Graves in his *Dictionary of Artists* gives his speciality as landscape. McCloy worked in both oils and watercolours, but the latter was his favourite medium. He was a very versatile artist. His work comprised domestic scenes, pictures of children, still life subjects and landscapes. He is best known for his child studies and domestic scenes which were popular with the Victorians. It has been said that his work indicated a limited ability as a figure painter. In Eileen Black's opinion, however: 'his true genius lay in landscape painting … a little-known side of his work. Finely and delicately executed, with close attention paid to detail and atmosphere, [these paintings] reveal him to have been a landscape painter of great merit and sensitivity.' His last exhibiting year in London was 1891. He was still a member of the Belfast Art Society in 1895. Samuel McCloy died at 117 Fernlea Road,

'The Bather' Exhibited Lisburn Museum. 1981/2.
(RWP)

Balham, on the 4 October 1904, in his seventy-third year. He had been in delicate health for about a year and had been unable to work.

An exhibition in Lisburn Museum, from 4 December 1981 – 26 February 1982, is believed to be the first exhibition ever held of McCloy's work. The Museum was officially opened in April 1981 and the catalogue of the exhibition, prepared by Eileen Black of the Ulster Museum's Art Department, was Publication No. 1, the first for the Museum. Samuel McCloy's work has become much sought after, after years of comparative neglect. Works by him can be found in the Victoria and Albert Museum, London, the National Museum of Wales, Cardiff, the National Gallery of Ireland, Dublin, the Ulster Museum, Belfast, and the Lisburn Museum; also in many private collections in Ireland and elsewhere.

Brigadier-General John Nicholson

(JSH)

JOHN NICHOLSON, THE SON of an Irish physician, Dr. Alexander Nicholson, was born in Dublin on 11 December 1822. His father died when he was nine years old, and his mother moved to Lisburn. He was educated at the Royal School Dungannon from 1834–38 and in 1839 became an ensign in the Indian army. In 1847, he became assistant to Sir Henry Lawrence, Resident at Lahore, and he distinguished himself in the Sikh war of 1848. When he was only twenty-eight years old he was appointed Deputy Commissioner of the Lahore Board. Throughout his career he was feared for his foul temper and authoritarian manner, but also gained the respect of the Afghan and North Punjabi tribes in the area for his fairhandedness and sense of honour. He was Governor of the Punjab for several years, and by 1857, the year of the Indian mutiny, he had been promoted to the rank of colonel and was stationed at Peshawar. He fought ferociously and was said to have been in the saddle for twenty hours during one battle. Having won various victories against the mutineers, he was soon appointed brigadier-general. He led a column to the relief of Delhi and organised an attack via the Kashmir Gate. The assault was successful, but Nicholson was mortally wounded and died on 23 September 1857, in a small bungalow in the cantonments of Delhi.

John Nicholson's remains were borne on a gun-carriage to a grave opposite the Kashmir Gate where the funeral service was read by the Rev. Mr Rotton, the chaplain to the Force. There was no pomp or show to mark the passing of India's greatest soldier; no cannon saluted the dead; no band played solemn music; no volleys of musketry rattled over the open grave – the small army had too much work in hand, both inside and outside the captured city, to pay the customary honours to the dead – but Nicholson was not forgotten. Nicholson's friends in India set up a tablet to his memory in the church at Bann. The inscription referred to his latest deeds and spoke of the man himself.

The Nicholson statue in its new position adjacent to Lisburn Museum.
(JSH)

> Gifted in mind and body, he was as brilliant in government as in arms. The snows of Ghazni attest his useful fortitude; the songs of the Punjab his manly deeds; the peace of this frontier his strong rule. The enemies of his country know how terrible he was in battle, and we his friends have to recall how gentle, generous, and true he was.

A much more visible monument was the plain obelisk on the crest of the Margalla Pass, which cuts through the ridge that rises across the road from Hasan Abdal to Rawalpindi –

Nicholson Monument, Margalla Pass.

with a small tank of water constructed in the pass below. The column was 'erected by friends British and Native' to a man who played a hero's part in four great wars for the defence of British India. He was 'Mourned by the two races with an equal grief.' John Nicholson's memory was recorded in popular folklore in the words of a ballad, chanted in Punjabi, by wandering minstrels in the streets of Delhi. During his lifetime Nicholson was idolized by the natives and in 1849 a Gosain or Hindu devotee discovered in Nicholson a reincarnation of the Brahmanic godhead and began to preach the worship of his new god Nikalsain. Many natives embraced the new creed and the sect of Nikalsainis was established. Their main persecutor was Nicholson, the divinity whom they adored – he rewarded his worshippers with floggings and imprisonment, but they took their punishment like martyrs and the more they suffered at his hands, the louder they chanted their hymns in honour of the mighty Nikalsain.

There are statues of Nicholson in Lisburn and Dungannon. The Lisburn statue depicting him, sword-wielding, in the thickest of the fighting, was designed by F. W. Pomeroy and was a gift to the town from Lisburn born, Henry Musgrave. Musgrave unfortunately died a few weeks before it was unveiled by Field-Marshal Sir Henry Wilson in January 1922. Nicholson's statue has recently retreated from the centre of Market Square to a position on the flank of the Museum. This unprecedented withdrawal was forced by an overwhelming spread of illuminated environmental improvements advancing undercover of rusting linen webs, their rear supported by weaver's aluminium ladders. After Indian independence Nicholson's statue, which stood at the Kashmir Gate in Delhi, was removed. It was preserved and eventually brought back to Ireland and erected in the grounds of the Royal School Dungannon. It was unveiled by Lord Mountbatten in April 1960 who said: 'I well remember the statue when it stood in Delhi, and it is a triumph that it will stand here in future.' To help defray some of the costs incurred a 5-a-side football tournament was held to support the Nicholson Statue Fund, with celebrities in attendance on each of the three nights.

Storming of the breach, Kashmir Bastion, relief mural in Lisburn Cathedral. *(JSH)*

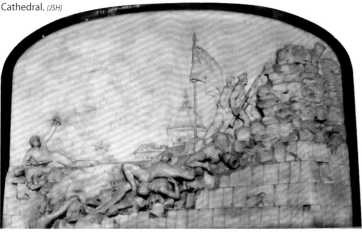

The Lisburn statue will be familiar to a passer-by, but many will be unaware of the relief tablet, designed and executed by J.H. Foley, R.A., which was placed by Nicholson's mother in the Cathedral. On the upper part of this memorial tablet, carved in clear relief on the white marble, is a scene which represents the storming of the breach in the Kashmir Bastion by Nicholson and his Fusiliers. Beneath the carved work runs the following inscription supplied by Sir Herbert Edwards:

The grave of Brigadier-General Nicholson, C.B., is beneath the fortress which he died to take. This monument is erected by his mother to keep alive his memory and example among his countrymen. Comrades who loved and mourn him add the story of his life: – He entered the army of the H.E.I.C. in 1839, and served in four great wars – Afghanistan, 1841–42; Satlaj, 1845–46; Punjab, 1848–49; India, 1857. In the first he was an Ensign; in the last a Brigadier-General and Companion of the Bath; in all a hero. Rare gifts had marked him for great things in peace and war. He had an iron mind and frame, a terrible courage, an indomitable will. His form seemed made for an army to behold; his heart, to meet the crisis of an empire; yet was he gentle exceedingly, most loving most kind. In all he thought and did, unselfish, earnest, plain and true; indeed, a most noble man. In public affairs, he was the pupil of the great and good Sir Henry Lawrence, and worthy of his master. Few took a greater share in either the conquest or government of the Punjab; perhaps none so great in both. Soldier and civilian, he was a tower of strength; the type of the conquering race. Most fitingly in the great siege of Delhi he led the first column of attack and carried the main breach. Dealing the death blow to the greatest danger that ever threatened British India, most mournfully, most gloriously, in the moment of victory, he fell mortally wounded on the 14th, and died on the 23rd of September 1857, aged only 34.

The East India Company acknowledged the debt they owed to Nicholson by granting his mother a special pension of £500 a year. Mrs. Nicholson endowed money for the building of the Nicholson Memorial Endowed School in memory of her children. The school was built adjacent to Christ Church in 1864.

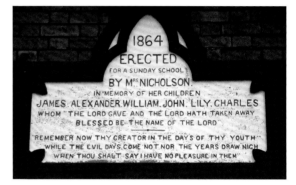

Memorial plaque on the wall of the school. dated 1864. *(JSH)*

Nicholson Memorial Endowed School, now part of Christ Church Lisburn. *(JSH)*

Lisburn Victoria Crosses

Two soldiers who were awarded the highest honour for bravery, the Victoria Cross, are commemorated with plaques on the base of the Nicholson statue in Market Square, Lisburn.

Corporal William James Lendrim VC

William James Lendrim (1830–1891) came from a military family and was born on New Year's Day, 1830 at Carrick-on-Shannon, Co. Leitrim, where his father, who was originally from Lisburn, was serving at that time. In 1845, he enlisted in the Royal Sappers and Miners, aged 15, as a bugler. He was posted to the Crimea on the outbreak of the conflict in 1854. He performed numerous acts of gallantry during that war and has the distinction that the award of the Victoria Cross was for three separate actions. The citation reads:

> Intrepidity – getting on the top of a Magazine, and extinguishing sandbags which were burning, and making good the breach under fire, on the 11th April 1855. For courage and praiseworthy example in superintending 150 French Chasseurs, on the 14th February 1855, in building No 9 Battery, Left Attack, and replacing the whole of the capsized gabions under a heavy fire. Was one of four volunteers for destroying the farthest Rifle Pit on the 20th April.

William Lendrim's medals.

The Victoria cross was presented by Queen Victoria on 26 June 1857 at Hyde Park, London. Corporal Lendrim was also present at the Battle of Lucknow during the Indian Mutiny. He later achieved the rank of Sergeant-Major and worked at the Staff College, Frimley. He died on the 28 November 1891, and is buried at the Royal Military Academy Cemetery at Sandhurst. His Victoria Cross is in the collection of the Royal Engineers' Museum, Chatham.

Sergeant Samuel Hill VC

Samuel Hill (1826–1863) was born in the village of Glenavy, close to Lisburn. He enlisted in 1844 and transferred in 1856 to the 90th Perthshire Light Infantry. His Victoria Cross was won at Lucknow in India in 1857. The citation reads:

> On 16th and 17th November 1857 at Lucknow, India, Sergeant Samuel Hill saved the life of a Captain (Irby) at the storming of Sedundra Bagh and also went under heavy fire to help two wounded men. In fact, he acted with gallantry throughout the operation for the Relief of the Lucknow Garrison.

Sergeant Hill died on the 21 February 1863 while on service in India.

Lieutenant William Dobbs

John Paul Jones.

Lieutenant William Dobbs was a son of the Rev. Richard Dobbs, Rector of Lisburn Cathedral from 1743 until 1775. William Dobbs lost his life at a naval battle in Carrickfergus Bay on 26 April 1778, against the celebrated Paul Jones, who was in command of the *Ranger*. Lieutenant Dobbs was not a member of the original crew of *H.M.S. Drake*, which was engaged in the battle; he was, apparently a visitor at Castle Dobbs and had been married just three days previously. He had volunteered for service. His memory is perpetuated by a beautiful mural monument in Lisburn Cathedral. A ballad describing the fight is preserved in the *Dublin University Magazine*, 1832. The ballad was partly suggested by a passage from a letter of Paul Jones to Lady Selkirk, dated Brest, 8 May 1778 and partly by tradition. The first and last stanzas give a flavour of the work.

> Paul Jones, the Pirate captain, has left the Scottish strand,
> And turned his blood-stained bows across to emerald Ireland;
> The roaring Mull of Galloway and the Copelands he has pass'd,
> And, Bangor on his weather beam, has opened Loch Belfast;
> But from the frightened fishermen the pirate stood away,
> And bore down on the anchored Drake in Carrickfergus Bay.
>
> And heaped about her silent guns–for, at the bloody post
> That each man held while living, he there gave up the ghost–
> Lay, soaked in sanguine uniform, the jackets of the blue,
> And the gay attire of gentry, and the homely hoddin too;
> And, doubled all across his gun upon the larboard bow,
> Lies Dobbs, the lit match in his hand–it cannot burn him now!

The following is an account of the engagement by Samuel McSkimin in a *History of Carrickfergus.*

The *Ranger*, an American vessel, commanded by the celebrated Paul Jones, arrived at the entrance to Carrickfergus Bay, and hoisting signal for a pilot, a fishing boat belonging to the Scotch-quarter went alongside, the crew of which were immediately made prisoners. These men Jones examined separately, respecting the force of the garrison and the number of guns carried by the *Drake,* an armed vessel then lying opposite the Castle; and being informed of her force, he lay off till night, when he entered the bay with an intention to board the *Drake* by surprise. Flood tide and a brisk gale during a snow shower, prevented his laying his *Ranger* alongside the *Drake;* on which he left the bay, and proceeded to Whitehaven. He landed there at 12 o'clock on the night of the 22nd with about fifty men, spiked the guns on the batteries, burned several vessels in the harbour, and retired without the loss of a man. At 10 o'clock on the morning of the 23rd he arrived off St. Mary's Isle, near Kirkcudbright, and landed

The engagement between the *Drake* and the *Ranger* off Carrickfergus.

with about forty men, intending to take Lord Selkirk prisoner; but learning that his lordship was from home, he walked for some time on the beach, while his lieutenants and men visited the castle of Lord Selkirk, and demanded his plate; which was delivered to them by Lady Selkirk.

Early on the morning of the 24th he again appeared at the entrance to Carrickfergus Bay. The *Drake* had sent out a boat, with an officer and six men to reconnoitre; but they were captured by the *Ranger,* off Black Head. Soon after, the *Drake* bore down upon the *Ranger*, and an engagement ensued, about mid-channel. Captain Burden, who commanded the *Drake,* was killed early in the action; Lieutenant Dobbs, second in command, was mortally wounded and the vessel being much cut up in her rigging, the men, who were mostly young hands, got into confusion, and she was forced to strike to the *Ranger,* after an action of one hour and fifteen minutes. The *Drake* had two men killed, and twenty-five wounded; the *Ranger* three killed and five wounded. The comparative force of the vessels, with respect to guns, was nearly equal. The *Drake* carried twenty guns, four pounders: the *Ranger* eighteen six pounders, besides swivels. On board the *Ranger* were 155 able seamen, some of whom were Irishmen – one a native of Carrickfergus: *Drake* had fewer hands, most of whom were ordinary seamen. Shortly after the action, Paul Jones liberated the fishermen, giving them a boat with provisions to carry them home, and also the main-sail of the *Drake.* On his arrival at Brest, Lord Selkirk's plate was sold for the benefit of the captors; but it was bought in by Paul Jones, who in March 1785, returned it all safe to Lord Selkirk and even paid for its carriage home.

The marble relief monument in Lisburn Cathedral is by the celebrated stone cutter Edward Smyth, who became famous for his 'finely wrought' work such as in the memorial to Lieutenant Dobbs.

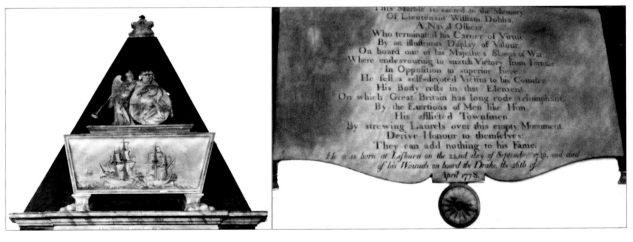

Monument to Lieutenant William Dobbs in Lisburn Cathedral. *(JSH)*

The inscription reads:

This marble is sacred to the
memory of Lieutenant William Dobbs.
A Naval Officer
Who terminated his career of virtue
By an illustrious display of valour
On board one of His Majesty's sloops of War
When endeavouring to snatch Victory from Fortune
In opposition to superior force
He fell a self-devoted victim to his country.
His body rests in that element
On which Great Britain has long rode triumphant
By the exertions of men like him.
His afflicted Townsmen
By strewing laurels over his empty monument
Derive honour to themselves
They can add nothing to his fame.

Lord Roberts' Oak, 1903

IN SEPTEMBER 1903, FIELD Marshal Lord Roberts travelled from Belfast to Lisburn to fulfill an onerous list of engagements. Field Marshal Lord Roberts of Kandahar, Pretoria and Waterford VC, KG, KP, GCB, OM, GCSI, GCIE., the 'Wellington of the Victorian era' was accompanied by Lieutenant-Colonel Phipps Hornby, V.C., and Lieutenant Colonel Wilson. Fog signals were detonated at Lambeg to herald his arrival and at Lisburn station he received an address from the Urban District Council. In reply Lord Roberts stated that for many years he had wished to visit Lisburn to see the birth place of the man for whom he had the most profound respect and admiration – General Nicholson – a man who was known throughout India, and who had extraordinary influence and power over the wild tribes of the north-west frontier of that country. (Nicholson was born in Dublin.) He continued:

Field Marshal
Lord Roberts.

It was my great privilege to serve for a short time on General Nicholson's staff and I perhaps had opportunities which few others had of understanding his great military genius and of appreciating his many noble qualities. General Nicholson did great things at Delhi and gave up his life there in defense of his country. I am proud to think that I was a soldier with General Nicholson.

T.R. Johnston-Smyth window in Christ Church, Lisburn. *(FGW)*

Lord Roberts visited the Cathedral and having viewed the Nicholson memorial he was directed to a memorial tablet in memory of Major Thomas Roger Johnson-Smyth, who served in South Africa with the Natal Field Force. Major Johnson-Smyth was killed in action during the Boer War, while leading his men of the 68th Regiment, 1st Battalion, Durham Light Infantry at the action of Vaalkrans on the Upper Tugela River, on 5 February 1900. Lord Roberts remembered the action. The Johnston-Smyth family lived at Ingram, Harmony Hill, Lambeg. At the request of the *Lisburn Standard*, Samuel Kennedy Cowan, the Lisburn poet, wrote a poem entitled *In Memoriam* to commemorate his death.

A great crowd had gathered in the Castle Gardens, adjoining the Cathedral where Lord Roberts had promised to plant a tree in memory of his visit. Can you believe all you read in newspapers? The *Belfast News Letter* informed its readers that Lord Roberts was received by the chairman of the parks committee, George B. Wilkins, and amid great enthusiasm his Lordship threw a few spadesful of mould on a healthy-looking specimen of black American spruce (*cryptomeria viridis*); after his departure Mr. Wilkins planted a tree in Wallace Park in commemoration of Earl Roberts' visit. The *Irish News & Belfast Morning News* only made mention of a tree planted in Wallace Park by the parks committee chairman. We follow this fiction with Fact – a plaque in Castle Gardens states: 'Lord Roberts Oak. Sept. 1903' and we can confirm that it is an oak tree.

Lord Roberts had long campaigned for more to be done for ex-servicemen, especially those who had been disabled. He took a keen interest in workshops for ex-servicemen and became one of the Trustees. Following his death in 1914, while visiting troops in France, it was decided, as a memorial to him, to expand the workshops and to name them after him. By 1920 there were eleven Lord Roberts Memorial Workshops around the country producing a wide variety of goods including basket ware, toys, beds and bedding and all types of furniture.

(JSH)

Brigadier John Alexander Sinton V.C., F.R.S.

BRIGADIER JOHN ALEXANDER SINTON had the unique distinction of being the only holder of the Victoria Cross who was also a Fellow of the Royal Society. He was born in Victoria, British Columbia, Canada, on 2 December 1884, the son of Walter Lyon Sinton and his wife Isabella Mary née Pringle, a family of Quaker linen manufacturers originally from the Ravarnette area. He was a grandson of Mr. and Mrs. John Sinton of Castle Street, Lisburn. In 1890 the family returned to Ulster. John Sinton's education began at the Nicholson Memorial School, Lisburn, now Christ Church Parochial Hall, and he then moved to the Royal Belfast Academical Institution from 1899 to 1902. He read Medicine at Queen's College, Belfast and graduated in 1908 being first in his year. He continued his studies obtaining degrees at the University of Cambridge and the University of Liverpool. He entered the Indian Medical Service in 1911.

During the First World War Sinton served in Mesopotamia with an Indian Cavalry Regiment and was awarded the Victoria Cross for most conspicuous bravery and devotion to duty during an action at Shiekh Sa'ed in 1916. The citation records the action:

> Although shot through both arms and the side he refused to go to hospital and remained as long as daylight lasted, attending to his duties under very heavy fire. In three previous actions Captain Sinton displayed the utmost bravery.

He was also mentioned in dispatches on four occasions and was awarded the Russian Cross of St. George. In 1919, Queen's University conferred the honorary degree of Doctor of Medicine 'in recognition of his early distinctions and of his valour in the field while engaged in the treatment and succour of the wounded'. Sinton was promoted brevet major in 1919 and after the armistice, while on active service in Afghanistan and Waziristan, he was mentioned twice in dispatches. In 1921 he was awarded an O.B.E.

Following the end of the war he left the army and joined the civil branch of the Indian Military Service. From 1921 to 1930 he oversaw the Quinine and Malaria Inquiry under the newly formed Central Malaria Bureau. He was director of the Malaria Survey of India from 1927 to 1936 and during this time he was also a member of the Malaria Commission of the League of Nations and undertook several epidemiological surveys on its behalf. On the outbreak of the Second World War he was recalled for active service and after a brief period in India he was successively consultant malariologist to the East African Forces,

Dr. Sinton administering aid to his injured comrades while under heavy fire. Mesopotamia 1916.
(Image courtesy of Museum of Melitary Medicine)

Revolver belonging to
Captain J.A. Sinton
*(Image courtesy of the
Inniskillings Museum,
Enniskillen)*

the Middle East Forces and the War Office.

He retired with the honorary rank of brigadier and returned to Northern Ireland at Cookstown. In his retirement he served as a Magistrate (JP) for Co. Tyrone, High Sheriff for that county in 1953 and Deputy Lieutenant in 1954. In 1946, he was elected a Fellow of the Royal Society for his work as a malariologist; his qualification to become a member reading:

It is doubtful if any other author during the last thirty years, has contributed more largely and importantly to scientific knowledge of malaria or has worked more originally and assiduously to advance such knowledge.

The memory of Brigadier Sinton's military service and commitment to saving life, lives on. The Sinton Medical and Dental Centre at Thiepval Barracks, Lisburn, replaces the centre destroyed by an IRA bomb on 7 October 1996, when a car bomb went off in the afternoon, followed by a second ten minutes later near the base's medical unit where victims had gathered. Warrant Officer James Bradwell was killed and 21 soldiers and 10 civilians were injured. At Queen's University, where Sinton was a member of the Senate and a Pro-Chancellor, a student housing block called 'Sinton Halls', is named in his memory. He may also be unique in having three mosquitoes named after him. Brigadier Sinton died at his home, 'The Lodge', Lough Fea, on 25 March 1956 and was buried with full military honours at Claggan Presbyterian Church cemetery in Cookstown. His Victoria Cross is displayed at the Museum of Military Medicine, Aldershot.

The Sinton medals
(MMM)

Thomas Andrews and Helen Reilly Barbour

IN JUNE 1908, HELEN Reilly Barbour, daughter of John Doherty Barbour of Conway, married Thomas Andrews, son of the Rt. Hon. J. Andrews of Comber, Co. Down. The wedding in Lambeg Parish Church was a magnificent occasion. Helen, or Nellie as she was known in the family, had seven bridesmaids and a pageboy attendant. She is said to have had two earnest suitors for her hand, Thomas Andrews and Henry Pierson Harland, a nephew of Sir Edward Harland.

A family story tells of an occasion when Nellie's mother locked her in her room and threatened not to let her out again until she had decided whether to marry Thomas or Henry. She chose Thomas. Thomas Andrews was the managing director and chief designer of Harland and Wolff and the designer of the *Titanic*. Their home was 'Dunallon' in Windsor Avenue, Belfast. They had one daughter, Elizabeth Law Barbour, who died unmarried, in a road accident in 1973.

Thomas Andrews sailed from Belfast on board the *Titanic* on 2 April 1912, en route for Southampton and the maiden voyage to New York. He was lost at sea on 15 April when the ship collided with an iceberg in mid-Atlantic. A *Titanic* survivor, Mary Sloan, a stewardess, wrote in a letter to her sister, 'He was a brave man. Mr Andrews met his fate like a true hero realising the great danger, and gave up his life to save the women and children of the *Titanic*. They will find it hard to replace him.' Helen, his widow, did eventually marry Henry Pierson Harland in 1916.

In Lambeg graveyard this tragic story is inscribed on a marble slab in the Barbour family plot:

In Loving Memory of
Helen Reilly
Daughter of John D. Barbour
of Conway, Dunmurry
Born 10th April 1881
Died 22nd August 1966
Married Thomas Andrews 1908
Lost RMS Titanic April 1912
"Heroic unto Death"
Married Henry Harland 1916
Died August 1945
Semper Vigilans

The wedding photographer on the day was the renowned Robert John Welch (1859–1936). His comment on the print overleaf can be seen bottom right. Welch was born in Strabane and his early interest in photography increased when he moved to Belfast

Entry from Marriage
Register of Lambeg
Parish Church, 24
June 1908.

and trained under E.T. Church. He set up business in 1883 in Lonsdale Street. He was commissioned by the Royal Commission of Enquiry in 1886 to record the damage caused in Belfast after the anti-Home Rule riots of that year. He was appointed official photographer to the firm of Harland & Wolff, and the Belfast Ropeworks Co. He was a member of the Royal Irish Academy, President of the Belfast Naturalist's Field Club and President of the Conchological Society of Great Britain and Ireland. Queen's University conferred an honorary doctorate in 1923 and the Northern Ireland Parliament granted him a civil pension in 1927. He died on 28 September 1936.

The wedding of Thomas Andrews, son of the Rt Hon J. Andrews of Comber and Miss Helen Barbour, daughter of John D. Barbour of Conway took place at Lambeg Parish Church on 24 June 1908. There were six bridesmaids and the bride's train was carried by Master Jack Andrews and Miss Rebecca Barbour.

(PRONI D/3655/A/6/1)

(PRONI D/3655/A/6/2)

Lisburn War Memorial

THE LISBURN WAR MEMORIAL stands in a commanding position in Castle Street at the entrance to the Castle Gardens, which provide a fitting background for a memorial. The figure, a bronze by Henry Charles Fehr (1867–1940), consists of the winged figure of Victory, carrying a down-pointed sword and a laurel wreath. The overall height of the memorial is twenty-three feet. The bronze figure is nine feet high and is mounted on a pedestal and steps of Bottacino marble. Set on the upper part of the pedestal are four bronze tablets; three are inscribed with the names of the fallen in the Great War; the other with the following inscription:

> To the Glorious Memory of the Lisburn Men
> who gave their Lives that we might live.
> 1914–1918.
> Their Name Liveth for Evermore.

A war memorial for Lisburn was first proposed in 1918 at the end of the war; however, it took until 1923 before a permanent memorial was finally in place. The unveiling ceremony on 28th April, was carried out by Major-General Sir Oliver Nugent, who was a former commander of the Ulster Division. In his remarks, Sir Oliver, a southern Unionist, was keen to heal the differences between nationalists widened by the recent War of Independence in Ireland and encouraged his audience to 'always remember the days when every man who fought on the same side was a brother.' A service was held in Castle Street, attended by Northern Ireland's first Prime Minister, Sir James Craig, local dignitaries, and ex-servicemen with their families. Colonel Pakenham, Commander of the 11th Battalion Royal Irish Rifles, called aloud the names of the 266 men inscribed on the memorial – silence – the haunting strains of the Last Post, played by buglers of the visiting Seaforth Highlanders, chilled the air.

Though November 1918 had marked the end of fighting on the Western Front, negotiations continued at the Paris Peace Conference until 1920, 'with the high and tremendous task of settling the peace terms.' The Treaty of Versailles was not signed until June 1919. Once negotiations were nearing their end and 'proper peace' was within sight, a peace committee was set up with the intention of deciding how Britain would publicly mark the end of the war and do justice to the widespread feelings

Lisburn War Memorial.
(JSH)

The Cenotaph in Market Square. *(ILC & LM)*

of jubilation. The committee at first considered a four-day August celebration, but this was simplified and reduced to a single day, under the direction of David Lloyd George, Prime Minister. Known as Peace Day – in Lisburn, Saturday, 16th August 1919 was the day appointed. To celebrate Peace Day a wooden cenotaph was erected in the middle of Market Square. This temporary memorial was based on the design for the cenotaph in Whitehall, London, which was also a temporary wood and plaster construction. Another made from Portland stone replaced it in 1920, which still stands today. The Market Square memorial was built by Ezekiel Bullick, the owner of a local joinery firm. The political position of Ireland in 1919 was fragile and national Peace Day celebrations were among the problems faced by returning nationalist servicemen. Thomas Kettle, professor, lawyer, journalist, poet and nationalist MP, realised the ambiguity of his position as a soldier in the British Army. His words indicate that he was acutely aware of how the public memory might subsequently be fashioned: 'These men [Easter 1916] will go down in history as heroes and martyrs, and I will go down – if I go down at all – as a bloody British officer.'

A procession of sailors and soldiers, school children, and representatives of public bodies and trades' organisations was the outstanding feature of the day. The procession was led by the children. There were about 3,000 of them and amongst them hundreds of miniature Union Jacks had been distributed, which they waved vigorously as they passed the saluting base outside the Assembly Rooms, where a platform, decorated with flags and streamers, had been erected for local dignitaries. Mr. J. Milne Barbour, who wore the uniform of a Deputy Lieutenant, acknowledged the salute of the children. The streets were ablaze with colour, there was a profusion of flags and bunting on every side. The whole of the route was lined with spectators. In the parade, the massed flags of the Allied nations were carried by a party of Boy Scouts; a number of Girl Guides and a detachment of the Church Lads' Brigade were also in the parade. The Naval representatives headed the ex-service men, the majority of whom wore civilian dress. They marched with splendid alignment, and were cheered by the crowds. The salute was taken by Brigadier-General Sir William Hacket Pain. The parade was viewed from the balcony of the Assembly Rooms by a number of disabled soldiers. After the officers and men of the Navy and Army came the V.A.D.s and other war nurses, the urban councillors, and representatives of local branches of trade unions. The rear of the procession was brought up by a fleet of decorated motor cars. The band of the 1st Battalion Norfolk Regiment, the Lisburn Silver Band and the Flute Band joined in the march. The school children went to Sandy Lane field, where they were entertained to tea and games, and the sailors and soldiers, who numbered about 800, marched to the Grain Market, where they were entertained to lunch.

At a luncheon to conclude the day's proceedings, the Chairman proposed the toast 'The Navy and Army.' He paid a warm tribute to our sailors and soldiers, and said if it had not been for their heroism and endurance the war might have ended differently. Brigadier-General Sir William Hacket Pain, in his reply, reminded his audience that this was not the first time he had visited Lisburn. He had the honour to command the 108th Brigade, which included the 11th Battalion Royal Irish Rifles, and as he looked at the parade that day and watched the men of the battalion passing, he thought of the days at Clandeboye and Aldershot and in France, where they had drilled, manoeuvred, and marched together, and he thought, too, of the many good men who were with them no more. Out of a population of 13,000, no fewer than 2,500 men from Lisburn enlisted in the Navy and Army, and of that number 500 laid down their lives. That was a large proportion, and the majority were men who served in the 11th Battalion R.I.R.

The Brigadier General, in his speech made no reference to a great victory. As an officer in the high command, he knew the volatile fortunes of battle had swung in our favour and he had full knowledge of the horrors of the conflict. He continued:

Thomas Kettle monument, St. Stephen's Green, Dublin. The bronze bust by A.G. Power RHA was erercted in 1937. *(RWP)*

> We had finished this war successfully, but he did not think anyone present really knew how near we were to losing it. The war produced all sorts of extraordinary coincidences. To begin with, we had a policy of dual control in the field. There was no General to direct all the arrangements necessary to obtain victory, and the result was that there was a certain amount of indecision. Eventually this was remedied by the appointment of Marshal Foch as generalissimo, and he entirely changed the situation. To show how very near we were to disaster he might tell them that when the Germans made their great push in March last year there were running between Amiens and Paris 140 trains a day with troops and supplies. When the German guns were within about 9,000 yards of that railway

line those trains were reduced to seven a day. It was very easy to see, considering what we had to supply at the time, how very near disaster was facing us, from starvation if from nothing else. He often thought that if it were known more generally what a near shave, so to speak, we had in the war people would be a little more serious, and take more trouble in trying to repair the things that had gone wrong.

The Lisburn War Memorial, like those at Hilden and Hillsborough, was designed to serve as custodian of the public memory of those who gave their lives in the 'War to end all Wars'. History tells a different story: Lisburn War Memorial now commemorates the fallen in World War II, Korea (1950–1953), The Falkland's War (1982) and Afghanistan (2001–2014). A separate memorial commemorates members of the Ulster Defence Regiment, who were killed in service to Northern Ireland. We turn to a poem by Tom Kettle:

So here, while the mad guns curse overhead,
And tired men sigh, with mud for couch and floor,
Know that we fools, now with the foolish dead,
Died not for Flag, nor King, nor Emperor,
But for a dream, born in a herdsman's shed,
And for the Secret Scripture of the poor.

The Gift of Love, Tom Kettle, 1916

On 9 September 1916, Lieut. Tom Kettle led his company from the trench during the dawn offensive on Ginchy. He was killed almost immediately. The poem quoted above, *The Gift of Love,* written for his daughter Betty a few days before he died, captures the futility of his sacrifice and that of his comrades in the 16th (Irish) Division. On the occasion of the dedication of the Peace Tower at Messines, a site close to where the 36th (Ulster) and the 16th (Irish) Divisions fought side by side in 1917, the Taoiseach, Bertie Ahern, quoted the lines: 'Died not for flag, nor King, nor Emperor / But for a dream, born in a herdsman's shed / And for the Secret Scripture of the poor' – a collective cross-border mourning of Ireland's war dead.

Long Kesh Airfield

SITUATED ON THE OUTSKIRTS of Lisburn, at the former Long Kesh airfield, are two 'historic' World War II buildings, which were erected under the auspices of the Ministry of Aircraft Production for use by Short & Harland for the assembly of Stirling heavy bombers. When war was declared on 3 September 1939 there was only one military airfield in Northern Ireland. By 1943 there were twenty-seven. Four of these were in the Lisburn area, at Long Kesh, Maghaberry, Blaris and Sandy Bay on Lough Neagh. Each airfield was used for a variety of purposes, however Long Kesh, Maghaberry and Blaris shared a common aim.

In drawing up airfield development plans for Northern Ireland the Air Ministry planners had to meet a number of requirements. Foremost was the ability to respond to a possible German invasion of the United Kingdom through the 'back door' – the Republic of Ireland – and to react immediately with a British Army led counter offensive supported by appropriate air cover. In addition to the Lisburn airfields, Sydenham, in Belfast, was included in this role. A pre-war civil airport and now the site

Long Kesh hangars 1942.
(UAS)

of a rapidly expanding aircraft manufacturing facility, Sydenham was not an ideal location due to its vulnerability to air attack, as demonstrated on 15 August 1940, when Short & Harland's aircraft factory was bombed by the Luftwaffe and five Stirling bombers were destroyed on the production line. An urgent need was also identified for an emergency landing ground to which 'planes could be rapidly dispersed'. This was met by the simple expedient of taking over two large fields at Blaris, opposite the old graveyard. The ground had already been used for air displays or private flying and was a flat, firm, well-drained site with largely unobstructed approaches. It was brought into immediate use as a grass airstrip and, under the control of the Long Kesh base, it was used for gliding instruction by the Air Training Corps from 1942 until the end of the war.

It took longer to commission the airfield at Long Kesh and its satellite airfield at Maghaberry. Construction work did not commence until November 1940 and soon the erection of the buildings was complete, but the construction of the runways took much longer due to the large amount of drainage and excavation work required. The result was that both airfields were not officially opened until November 1941. As the war developed new roles were found for Long Kesh and Maghaberry and by 1 April 1942 the United States Navy commenced a thrice-weekly scheduled service between Eglinton and Hendon airfield, London, calling at Long Kesh to drop and collect passengers, light freight and mail.

On 26 August 1942, Long Kesh chalked up a novel achievement when the first Stirling

War Graves of twenty-six airmen from Great Britain and the Empire buried at All Saints, Eglantine, close to RAF Long Kesh. *(JSH)*

bomber produced by the Short & Harland assembly plant took off on a trial flight. The second Stirling to be produced was test-flown on 10 October and others followed in due course. Stirlings were also test-flown from Maghaberry, where another assembly plant had been constructed. Altogether 1,213 Stirling bombers were manufactured in Northern Ireland, out of the total of 2,371 built and flown in the United Kingdom. Ironically, in the immediate post-war period, several hundred Stirlings were stored at Maghaberry airfield prior to being scrapped and melted down. Tragically, not a single Stirling survives anywhere in the world, an unforgivable end to the career of the first four-engine heavy bomber to be built for and operated by the RAF in the Second World War. A new role for the Long Kesh and Maghaberry airfields came at the end of 1942, when they were taken over by Coastal Command No.17 Group for use by No.5 Operational Training Unit, whose function was to instruct pilots and crews on the operation of Beauforts and Hampden aircraft.

On the 17 July 1945, two Dakotas of RAF Transport Command, escorted by two squadrons of Mustang fighters, piloted by Poles, and by Warwick Aircraft of the Air Sea Rescue Service, touched down at Long Kesh, in brilliant sunshine, having left Northolt, Middlesex, exactly two hours and one minute earlier. As the leading aircraft taxied towards the waiting crowd, the Royal Standard was broken from its nose; this was the first royal visit to Northern Ireland by air. There were cheers from the crowd as the King, in the uniform of a Marshall of the Royal Air Force, came into view, followed by the Queen in a two-piece suit of dove grey with a matching hat with a royal blue bow. They were accompanied by the Princess Elizabeth in the work-a-day khaki of the ATS. This was a Victory visit to Ulster and for the Princess, her first flying experience. The RAF guard of honour gave the royal salute and the Royal Standard was slowly raised on the station flagpole. The Royal party spent the remainder of the day quietly at Government House, Hillsborough, and in the evening dined with the Governor and Duchess of Abercorn. Afterwards the party was 'entertained' by Lambeg drummers in the courtyard. Their Majesties spent two days at Hillsborough before continuing their journey by air to Eglinton, Co. Londonderry. Other distinguished visitors who passed through Long Kesh included General Eisenhower in August 1945 and Field Marshal Montgomery, one month later.

Royal Party arrives at Long Kesh. *(UAS)*

The Long Kesh aviation story continues. It is now home to the Ulster Aviation Society, which operates in the World War II hangars. We are indebted to Ernie Cromie, former Society chairman, for the content of this article. The Society has on display an extensive collection of more than thirty aircraft, which includes vintage WW II fighters, cold war era fast jet fighters, some Short Bros & Harland aircraft, military helicopters and civilian aircraft. The Society also has on exhibition, equipment, engines and other artefacts as well as rare aviation reference manuals, all with strong links to aviation within Ireland. This is a working society and visits are possible by prior arrangement, from March to November.

Aircraft belonging to the Ulster Aviation Society, on view at Long Kesh. Above, a SD3-30 civilian aircraft, left, a Canberra PR9, XH131. Both aircraft were built by Short Brothers, Belfast. *(UAS)*

Professor James Francis Pantridge

(ILC & LM)

JAMES FRANCIS 'FRANK' PANTRIDGE was born in Hillsborough on 3 October 1916. Educated at Friends' School, Lisburn, he graduated in medicine from Queen's University in 1939 and was commissioned in the Royal Army Medical Corps on the 12 April 1940. Captain Pantridge was awarded the Military Cross for his courageous action during the fall of Singapore to Japanese forces in February 1942; in Churchill's terms, the 'worst disaster and largest capitulation in British history'. Serving as a regimental medical officer with the Gordon Highlanders, Pantridge's conduct was exemplary, the citation reading:

This officer worked unceasingly under the most adverse conditions of continuous bombing and shelling and was an inspiring example to all with whom he came into contact. He was absolutely cool under the heaviest fire.

Professor Pantridge by John Sherlock. (JSH)

As a prisoner of war, he spent his captivity in the slave labour camps of the Burma-Siam railway, including some months in the Tanbaya death camp, where few survived. When he was liberated he was emaciated and had contracted cardiac beriberi, where protein deficiency damages the heart, which is usually fatal, and which may have ignited his interest in heart disease. He survived, but suffered ill health related to the disease for the rest of his life. His experience in the prison camps undoubtedly scarred him mentally as well as physically. He was appalled at the Japanese guards' cruelty, and approved Harry Truman's decision to drop the atomic bomb in August 1945, which saved POW's lives.

After the war he worked as a lecturer in the Pathology Department at Queen's University and then won a scholarship to the University of Michigan, where he studied under Dr. F.N. Wilson, then the world authority on electrocardiography. Frank Wilson was cardiologist to President Lyndon Johnson: later, Pantridge's defibrillator was used on Johnson when he had a heart attack. He returned to Belfast in 1950 and was appointed as cardiac consultant to the Royal Victoria Hospital and professor at Queen's University, where he remained until his retirement in 1982. There he established a specialist cardiology unit whose work was recognised worldwide.

By 1957, Pantridge and his colleague, Dr. John Geddes, had introduced the modern system of cardiopulmonary resuscitation (CPR) for the prompt treatment of cardiac arrest. Further study led Frank Pantridge to the realization that many deaths resulted from ventricular fibrillation which needed to be treated before the patient was admitted to hospital. This led to his introduction of the mobile coronary care unit, an ambulance with specialist equipment and staff to provide pre-hospital care. To extend the usefulness of initial treatment, Pantridge went on to develop the portable defibrillator, and in 1965 installed his first version in a Belfast ambulance. It weighed 70 kg and operated from car batteries, but by 1968 he had designed an instrument weighing only 3 kg, incorporating a miniature capacitor manufactured for NASA. Pantridge's refinement of the automated external defibrillator (AED) allowed it to be used safely by members of the public. Professor Frank Pantridge was awarded the CBE in 1978. He died, aged 88, on Boxing Day 2004. He never married. He was the author of *The Acute Coronary Attack* (1975), and a volume of autobiography, *An Unquiet Life* (1989). The City of Lisburn commissioned a bronze statue by John Sherlock which stands outside the council offices.

Acknowledgements

The authors would like to acknowledge the staff of the many organisations whose co-operation and assistance contributed to the compilation of this book. Amongst them the Wallace Collection, Lisburn Library, Queen's University, Ulster Museum, Lisburn Cathedral, British Newspaper Archive, Public Record Office of Northern Ireland, Neil Armstrong, curator of the Inniskillings Museum, David Wiggins of the Museum of Military Medicine, Fred Hall of Ballance House, Sarjeant Gallery Whanganui, Ernie Cromie and the Ulster Aviation Society. We appreciate the help and assistance of the Earl of Bathurst, Rev. Eddie Coulter, James Davidson, Jackie McQuillan, Tatch and the Andrews family. We have drawn from many sources and are grateful for the research that led to the articles published in historical society journals. The help and support of Malcolm and Wesley Johnston of Colourpoint Books was much appreciated. The encouragement of Vera and Mavis was greatly appreciated.

   Our especial thanks are due to the Irish Linen Centre and Lisburn Museum Curator Paul Allison and his staff for their assistance and support, in particular Trevor Hall, Ciaran Toal and Elaine Flanagan.

FG Watson, JS Hanna,
May 2018

Key to Photo Credits

BCL	*Belfast Central Library*
FGW	*F.G. Watson*
GG	*Rev. Dr. Gordon Gray*
HK	*Heather Kenny*
ILC & LM	*Irish Linen Centre & Lisburn Museum*
JSH	*J.S. Hanna*
MMM	*The Museum of Military Medicine*
PRONI	*Public Record Office of Northern Ireland*
QUB	*Queen's University Belfast*
RWP	*Richard Watson Photography*
UAS	*Ulster Aviation Society*

Select Bibliography

Ancient Monuments of Northern Ireland, vol. 1: in State Care, Belfast, 1926, HMSO

Bannister, R.C., & Hamilton, R.V., *Sport in Lisburn Past and Present*, Belfast, 1910

Bayly, Henry, *Topographical and Historical Account of Lisburn, also a Poem on the same The Maze – A Satire. To which is added some Miscellaneous Pieces*, Belfast, 1834

Bell, Henry, *A Short Visit to Ram's Island, Lough Neagh and its vicinity in the year 1853*, Belfast, 1853

Best, E.J. 'Health and Wealth in the Borough of Lisburn', 1979

Blair, May, *Once Upon the Lagan, The Story of the Lagan Canal*, Belfast, 1981

Black, Eileen, Samuel McCloy (1831–1904) *Subject and Landscape Painter* (Lisburn Museum, 1981–1982)

Brett, C.E.B., *Buildings of North County Down*, 2002

Brett, C.E.B. and Lady Dunleath, *List of Historic Buildings in the Borough of Lisburn*, Belfast, 1969

Burns, J.F. '*From Whoredom to Evangelism, The Story of Mrs Thistlethwayte*', 1979

'Coulsons of Lisburn' in *Belfast Municipal Museum and Art Gallery, Quarterly Notes*, 1938

Crawford, W. H., *Domestic Industry in Ireland*, Dublin, 1972

Cromie, Ernie, 'A Brief History of Lisburn's Air Bases', 2006

Day, Angélique & McWilliams, Patrick, editors, *Ordnance Survey Memoirs of Ireland, vol 8, Parishes of Co. Antrim II* 1832–8, Belfast, 1991

Diocese of Down & Connor archives. Letter dated 26 Jan. 1939 to William McIlroy signed E Cardinal Pacelli, Secretary of State, headed Pope Pius XI, proclaiming him a Knight of the Order of Saint Gregory.

Dixon, Hugh, '*So Many Proofs, Aspects of the legacy of Sir Richard Wallace in the fabric of Lisburn*', 1982

Foy, J.H., *Kilwarlin Moravian Church a Visitor's Guide*

Gilliland, Jean, *Gladstone's "Dear Spirit" Laura Thistlethwayte*, Oxford, 1994

Great Protestant Demonstration at Hillsborough, October 30, 1867, Authentic Report, 1867

Greene, W.J., *A Concise History of Lisburn and Neighbourhood*, Belfast, 1906

Hardy, P.D., *Twenty-One Views in Belfast and its Neighbourhood*, Dublin, 1837

Heaney, Mavis, *Lisburn, Life in the County Down*, Coleraine, 1996

Industries of the North One Hundred Years Ago, Belfast, 1986

Johnston, B., *Lisburn Cricket Club 1836–1986*, 1986

Johnston, J.G., Presidential address delivered to the Northern Ireland Branch of the British Medical Association, Oct. 1948

Kinealy, Christine, 'The Lisburn Workhouse during the Famine', 1991

Law, Isobel, A Tale of Two Churches, Two Centuries of Methodism at Priesthill: 1786–1986, Belfast, 1986

Lawlor, H.C., 'The Rise of the Linen Merchants', in Fibres & Fabrics Journal, 1941–1943

Lewis, Samuel, A Topographical Dictionary of Ireland, London, 1837

Mackey, Brian, Lisburn the Town and its People 1873–1973, Belfast, 2000

Magee, John, The Heritage of the Harp, The Linen Hall Library and the Preservation of Irish Music, Belfast, 1992

Maguire, W.A. Dr, (Editor), The Huguenots & Ulster 1685–1985, Lisburn Museum Exhibition Catalogue, Belfast, 1985

Marshall, H.C. Rev. The Parish of Lambeg, Lisburn, 1933

Minute Book of The Irish Harp Society, 1808–1810, Linen Hall Library

Moore, Alfred S., 'Ulster's First Railway', in the Belfast News Letter, 12 August 1939

McBride, I.R., Scripture Politics Ulster Presbyterians and Irish Radicalism in the Late Eighteenth Century, Oxford, 1998

McCall, Hugh, Ireland and her Staple Manufactures: being sketches of the history and Progress of the Linen and Cotton Trades, third edition, Belfast, 1870

McCarrison, J.H.F., Lisburn Golf Club 1905–1980, Lisburn, 1980

McClelland, Aiken, 'The Irish Harp Society' in Ulster Folklife, vol. 21, 1975

McIvor, Timothy, The Rainmaker, John Ballance 1839–1893, Auckland, 1989

McKinstry, Robert, 'Chrome Hill, Lambeg', 1987

Ó Baoill, Ruairí, 'Excavations at Castle Gardens, Lisburn', 2006

Patterson, E.M., The Great Northern Railway of Ireland, 1962

Pierce, Nicola, Lisburn, Phoenix from the Flames, Belfast, 2008

These Hallowed Grounds, Lisburn Branch of the North of Ireland Family History Society, vol. 1, Belfast, 2001, vol. 2, Belfast, 2005

The Lisburn Temperance Institute – Bridge Community Centre, 1890–1990

Vincent, Ian, 'New Life for an Egan Harp', 2006

Warner, Richard, 'The Lisburn Area in the Early Christian Period', 1989

Watson, F.G., 'The Racecourse' in Dromore and District Local Historical Group Journal, vol. 1, 1991. 'The Plight of the Cotton Weavers at Lisburn, Maze and Broomhedge in 1862–63' in Dromore and District Local Historical Group Journal, vol. 5, 1996

Watson, Fredrick Gilbert, All Around Lambeg, Belfast, 2008

Friends of the Cancer Centre

For over 30 years, Friends of the Cancer Centre has been dedicated to making a real and meaningful difference to cancer patients and their families across Northern Ireland.

Friends of the Cancer Centre enhances the quality of patient care and support through its life-changing and life-saving work which includes funding additional nurses, supporting local research and providing practical support, such as financial grants, which can help people through a really difficult time. Friends of the Cancer Centre relies entirely on the generosity of the local community. All money donated stays in Northern Ireland, directly benefitting patients and their families.

A board of trustees plays a vital role within the charity. Their role is not merely symbolic: they decide how to spend the available resources and which projects the charity funds. The board is made up of a diverse range of people from all sectors ensuring that the necessary expertise and knowledge is at hand to make such important decisions. This includes senior doctors from the Cancer Centre, leading business figures and some of the longest serving volunteers and fundraisers. They volunteer their time to ensure that the charity is governed correctly, and the money raised is used to its maximum potential to help patients.

Friends of the Cancer Centre has become an integral part of cancer services in Northern Ireland and it simply wouldn't be possible without the charity's supporters. These incredible people give up their valuable time to make a real and lasting difference to the charity. The late John Scott Hanna was one such volunteer fundraiser, and it is appropriate that royalties from the sale of *Lisburn, Past and Present – People, Places and Things* are donated to the charity in his memory. Many of the volunteers have been with the charity since its beginning thirty years ago and that volunteer base and support continues to grow. Friends of the Cancer Centre is always on the lookout for new volunteers who would like to give a little time – even a few hours – to help the charity. We invite you to find out more about volunteer opportunities.

Friends of the Cancer Centre
Northern Ireland Cancer Centre
Belfast City Hospital
Lisburn Road
BT9 7AB
info@friendsofthecancercentre.com
Tel: 028 9069 9393